PER ARDUA AD INFINITUM

John Dicks

MINERVA PRESS
MONTREUX LONDON WASHINGTON

PER ARDUA AD INFINITUM
Copyright © John Dicks 1995

All Rights Reserved

No part of this book may be reproduced in any form
by photocopying or by any electronic or mechanical means,
including information storage or retrieval systems,
without permission in writing from both the copyright
owner and the publisher of this book.

ISBN 1 85863 526 8

First published 1995 by
MINERVA PRESS
1 Cromwell Place
London SW7 2JE

Printed in Great Britain by
B.W.D. Ltd., Northolt, Middlesex

PER ARDUA AD INFINITUM

*A proportion of the profits from the sale
of this book have been donated to the
RAF Benevolent Fund*

CONTENTS

CHAPTER 1.	Enlistment, and Initial Training at Uxbridge Depot.	11
CHAPTER 2.	Service Life at a Flying Training School.	21
CHAPTER 3.	Remustering to Aero-engine Fitter. A year at a Technical Training Unit.	25
CHAPTER 4.	Life at another Flying Training Unit; this time as a technician.	31
CHAPTER 5.	RAF Hullavington. A move to a brand new airfield.	40
CHAPTER 6.	A real change of lifestyle. Life in an Aircraft Carrier, with all that that meant.	44
CHAPTER 7.	At sea on an Autumn cruise.	53
CHAPTER 8.	Ashore again; this time as a guest of the RAF at RAF Gosport.	59
CHAPTER 9.	Still ashore, but in Scotland.	70
CHAPTER 10.	Scapa Flow. How the Navy - and the RAF - reacted to the Munich Crisis. Some amusing aspects.	78
CHAPTER 11.	RAF Henlow; and War preparations.	91
CHAPTER 12.	Nantes and the B.E.F.	97
CHAPTER 13.	St. Nazaire and S.S. Floristan.	111
CHAPTER 14.	Norfolk, and an active Bomber squadron.	118

CHAPTER 15. Detachment to Malta with 18 Squadron. 130

CHAPTER 16. Escape from Malta to Cairo and the Western Desert. 141

CHAPTER 17. A light relief period with the Royal Egyptian Air Force. 151

CHAPTER 18. A move to Benghazi, and sundry adventures. 159

CHAPTER 19. Algiers; and the life of a factory-worker. 169

CHAPTER 20. Over to Italy, and a Salvage Unit at Udine. Intermissions in Austria. 178

CHAPTER 21. Homeward Bound, and some disillusionment with the Home Establishment of the RAF. 185

LIST OF ILLUSTRATIONS

Fig. 1.	Group of recruit squad, under training at Uxbridge, 1934.
Fig. 2.	Aerial view of Manston. RAF Station.
Fig. 3.	Osprey in "warpaint" and new type hangar at RAF Thornaby, 1935.
Fig. 4.	Internal view of barrack-room, Thornaby.
Fig. 5.	An Audax and an ambulance meet!
Fig. 6	Views of RAF Hullavington.
Fig. 7.	E.R.S. Furious.
Fig. 8.	H.M.S. Furious.
Fig. 9.	RAF Donibristle, Fife.
Fig. 10.	The author and his Raleigh M/C.
Fig. 11.	A cushy billet at Blickling Hall.
Fig. 12.	The crews of the last two Blenheims of 18 Sqdn. to leave Malta.
Fig. 13	18 Squadron ground staff at Sidi Barrani.

GLOSSARY

C.B.	Confined to Barracks (or Camp)
E.R.S.	Engine Repair Section (or Shop)
M.U.	Maintenance Unit
S.D.	Service Dress
Titfer	Tit for tat. Rhyming slang for peaked cap
P.T.I.	Physical Training Instructor
F.T.S.	Flying Training School
S. of T.T.	School of Technical Training
Buzz	A rumour
Bods } Erks }	Airmen in general
Colney Hatch	A 19th Century lunatic asylum in Kent
Dhobi	Laundry (Hindi)
Pawni	Water (Hindi)
Hoggin	The sea
E.P.I.P.	European Personnel India Pattern (A large tent about 20 feet square)
L.C.T.	Landing craft, Tank
R.T.O.	Railway Transport Officer (Army)

M.E.F.	Middle East Forces Command
R.E.A.F.	Royal Egyptian Air Force
N.A.A.F.I.	Navy, Army and Air Force Institute
E.N.S.A.	Entertainments National Service Association

CHAPTER 1
Uxbridge

"Well, cheerio, Mum! I'll see you tonight sometime," and off I went with a rail-warrant in my pocket, bound, as I thought, for a free day out in the Smoke, full of the excitement which anticipation engendered in my young and innocent breast.

It was the beginning of October in 1934, and this was the moment for which I had been waiting since my eighteenth birthday that summer. Actually, I had been waiting for much longer than that; there had been only one thought in my mind since I had first seen an aeroplane - and that had been to fly; the only way that that had seemed likely to be accomplished was by joining the RAF.

Having sat - and failed - both the Civil Service and RAF Boy-Entrant exams (failed because I had no knowledge of logarithms, trigonometry and such esoterics), I had just lived for the day that I should be eighteen and could join as a "man".

Luckily I was not a complete stranger to London, so I had no difficulty in finding Whitehall and the then RAF recruiting office in Gwydwr House, a fairly imposing building for such purposes perhaps, but we hopeful candidates didn't move in areas above the basement, which I remember as just a maze of dusty rooms with bare board floors.

I don't recall the exact sequence of our induction - there were seven or eight of us with this ambition to be "intrepid birdmen" - but there was an examination in basic maths and English, which included the writing of an essay: and there was a medical which was rather more exacting, one item of which amused me. The soles of my feet were anointed with iodine and a print made on sheets of white paper - flat feet were obviously not going to be permitted to pollute any RAF barrack square.

We must have been fed at some stage of the process, and when the Recruiting Office felt that they had eliminated all the undesirable characters, a gorgeously dressed sergeant, complete with highly decorative sash, gathered us together and - if our progress could really be so described - 'marched' us to an Underground Station, probably Green Park. Here we entrained and somehow the sergeant managed to keep us in one party until he had delivered us to what was then a recruits' reception centre and trade-testing unit at West Drayton: a place which nowadays houses one of the control centres of the civil aviation network.

"Ah, I thought, now we shall see some aeroplanes! This is what I came for." How wrong can one be? All we saw there were rows of huts, albeit some were of two storeys.

One of these huts we were taken to, and there we were introduced to the standard Macdonald, which was a steel-slatted bed of two sections, the lower, or foot end, of which was designed to slide under the head end so that it only took up half as much floor space. This was probably so that inspecting officers and other, sometimes unwelcome, visitors could move through the barrack-rooms with greater ease. The mattresses on these beds consisted of three square sections which we later learned to call "biscuits": not because of their hardness, which was not all that bad when one became used to them - and certainly more healthy than some modern beds - but because of their shape and colour. They were brown, thin, and square, just like the hardtack, which, with bully beef and Maconochie's meat and vegetables, was reputed to have been the staple diet for the lads in the trenches during the First World War.

Concerning bully beef, I'm reminded of an occasion when on cookhouse fatigues at Uxbridge. We were collecting rations from a storeroom when I noticed that the boxes of bully beef tins were dated 1917; nearly as old as I was! And incidentally, the beef was still wholesome and enjoyable, which says a great deal for the packers and the system.

However, still at West Drayton; after our first night on a Macdonald, we were sworn-in and signed up as Aircraftmen Second Class in the trade of Aircrafthand. "Good-ho," I thought, "that means I'll be working on aeroplanes soon," and, in fact, I actually saw one flying over Drayton that day, which, in my ignorance, I thought must have been from Uxbridge, where, we were told, we should be going next day.

More disappointments. The machine turned out from enquiries to have been from nearby Northolt. We found later that there was indeed an aircraft at Uxbridge; it was a Bristol Fighter F2B which was used to teach us tyro erks how to swing an airscrew for starting the engine without getting decapitated or otherwise upsetting the peaceful running of the RAF. This operation took four men, in theory; one in the cockpit to operate magneto switches and fuel cocks, and a team of three to swing the prop. After taking turns to turn the engine over to charge the cylinders with petrol vapour, one man grasped the propeller and the other pair held hands with him in line to help with the turning of the airscrew and to pull "No. 1" from the path of the prop when the engine fired. Actually, I once saw a flight-sergeant swing the prop of a Gladiator with one hand and it started first time, but he *DID* know what he was doing.

Our arrival at Uxbridge, after a short journey by road in the back of a three-tonner, and without the beautiful sergeant, was a little more intimidating than that at West Drayton - armed sentries at the gate, an imposing guardroom where we were checked in, and beautifully trimmed grass edging to spotless tarmac roads.

There was a barrack square with which we should get much closer acquainted during the coming three months, and this was surrounded by large buildings, several of which were living quarters; three storey barrack blocks with names of historical battles of the Middle East in the last War, like Kut and Megiddo. Appropriately named too, there was going to be a series of battles during that autumn and winter for us newly arrived rookies, most of which we were destined to lose!

It was to one of those exotically named blocks that we were taken and introduced to the corporal in charge of the barrack-room: an alarming figure, who turned out to be- our Drill Instructor; in retrospect, quite worthy of capital letters because he also proved to be our guide and mentor.

Then, was due allocation of bed-spaces, a very simple process; "In single file forward march, halt. Right turn; stand in front of the bed nearest to you, that's your bed." We were told to remember where it was, the number of the room, and the name of the barrack block.

Next step in our induction was the "kitting-out", and this proved to be much more complicated and long-drawn out. We marched - everywhere we marched - to what proved to be a clothing-store, and here were issued a multitude of items of clothing and equipment, which included two tunics with high collars fastened by hooks and eyes, five brass buttons down the front and more brass buttons on the breast pockets, not to mention a brass buckle to the belt. When one considers the eight buttons on our greatcoats, a cap badge, and all the brass-work on the canvas equipment that became such a trouble to us during the ensuing months, we must have boosted the sales of metal polish quite considerably.

In addition to all this blue serge gear, there were three blue cotton shirts - collarless in those days - three pairs of short underpants in a sort of cotton mixture fabric, three pairs of grey woollen socks - good stuff these - and an almost complete toiletry kit comprising towels, hair-brush, shaving ditto, two boot brushes and a clothes brush; these last I still use, with no apparent signs of wear having taken place in the last fifty-odd years! Nothing one can buy today would compare even faintly with such quality.

There was also a button-stick (a brass shield to slide under buttons when polishing them to keep Brasso off the cloth); and of course, the means of eating; knife, fork, spoon, and a pint porcelain mug. Even today I find the standard civvie cup holds hardly enough to be worthwhile drinking! There was also an item called a housewife - pronounced "hussif" - with no obvious use but which it was later discovered was intended to contain darning needles and wool etc., for repairs to issue garments. A compartmented item with the easily understood name of hold-all, and intended to do just that, was very useful at times. No razor was issued; if there had been, doubtless it would have been a cut-throat, no toothbrush either; and what might be called consumables - soap, polishes, toothpaste etc. - were to be our own responsibility, as also were pyjamas should we consider them necessary. Actually, they were available from the clothing stores on what was known as repayment - at the grand price of one shilling and sixpence per upper or lower garment.

The cap, which was intended to receive the aforesaid cap-badge, was not the funny little Glengarry of later years which always refused to stay put on my head - tending to slide round to look like a parody of Napoleon's tit-for-tat; but was the round peaked model, known as Cap, Service Dress, or SD for short. There were also two nether garments in the usual heavy serge, one pair of normal trousers and the necessary pair of braces to prevent their weight from bringing them down around the ankles; and a pair of what were described as pantaloons. Nothing whatever to do with any Shakespearean character these, but looking just like riding breeches without the knee strappings. There were puttees too, to be worn with the breeches - about three yards of cloth to be wound round the lower leg like a bandage, starting from the top inch-and-a-half of the boot and finishing just below the knee in such a manner that the stitch line where the puttee tapered off to the securing tape came exactly in line with the outer seam of the breeches leg. This was just the opposite way in which I had had to wear puttees (is that the right word to use about what one does with puttees?), in the Yeomanry. There we started at the knee and worked down to the boot with the tapes around the ankle. Perhaps the RAF way was the better, at least we didn't have to Blanco our blue tapes as the Army did their khaki ones!

And then the boots! Ah! How different these were from Army issue! Those were raw leather, liberally soaked in good dubbing. They would have been waterproof enough for a deep-sea diver had they been left alone; but we had to spend hours and several tins of Cherry Blossom to REMOVE the dubbing and make the boots shine - or else.

RAF boots weren't like that. They were already shiny, like new boots should be. They had soft leather uppers and rubber soles and heels - not a nail in them: the RAF had, and still has, a strong objection to its personnel striking sparks from the ground in the presence of explosive-filled aircraft and highly volatile aviation spirit. But there were no aircraft at Uxbridge, only that large barrack square, and we were marched with one of our nice new pairs of boots to the camp cobbler. There, this vandal tore off the nice rubber soles etc., and replaced them with thick leather ones, into which he proceeded to belt rows of heavy nails, steel toe-caps and steel heel-tips.

It seemed strange at the time, but there turned out to be a fairly good reason for this maniacal behaviour. When a file of soldiers - or airmen - is drilling, the general idea is for them to perform the movements together. As they cannot see each other because looking to the front is a first requirement except during special drills, such as saluting on the march or dressing (lining up of ranks), then some other means must be available - and the sound of heavily-nailed boots hitting gravel is just the job! Other sounds are made of course, like when a stiffly Blancoed rifle sling smacks against the well-polished stock of a Lee-Enfield 303 at the same instant as the right foot hits gravel during the Present Arms.

A rifle, of course, was another item issued to us at the Uxbridge Depot, but that turned out to be only a local issue for drill purposes, as also was the long bayonet with brass fittings to its black leather scabbard. An interesting combination this, having polished the leather with boot polish until it shone splendidly, the brass needed application of Brasso or Bluebell with the not uncommon result that the leather received some too. This mixture of polishing treatments was to be the bane of our lives until we were more expert in the art of the "Bull".

Blancoing the canvas of our equipment 'harness' - pack, belt, haversack, etc., and following that with polishing the brass buckles was a nightmare. There were occasions when, after some kit inspection parade, one might be told to do it again, but it was seldom as simple as that. Oh no! First, the whole kit had to be scrubbed clear of Blanco - which was a sort of grey clay - then it was re-inspected before reblancoing for the final - hopefully - inspection: sheer sadism!

The blade of the bayonet was something of a problem; emery cloth was not on the cards, as once scratched it would never polish well. In this matter I was lucky: when in the Yeomanry I had obtained a burnisher for polishing the steel scabbard and blade of my cavalry sabre; this burnisher was just a chain-mail epaulette sewn to a piece of leather, and was very effective, if hard graft. And talking of hard graft, those boots needed some considerable work on them to satisfy the demands of our drill instructors. These were mostly corporals, with a sergeant to keep THEM on their toes; and a Warrant Officer, who was - and probably still is - known as a Sergeant-Major. This last gentleman was in charge of all the recruit training of which there were several squads in various stages of progress towards becoming airmen; and he took on the aspect of a God to us lowly types - but not a god with much mercy either!

On the occasion of the many kit inspections, with which we were plagued at too frequent intervals, those boots had to shine like glass, soles, heels, and uppers; even the rubber-soled pair.

Everything we owned had to be laid out. The Macdonald beds were pulled out as if for sleeping on, the three biscuits covered by one of the blankets, which was tucked in neatly, with the other three folded so that they had the appearance of large books piled at the head of the bed. Our greatcoats were placed above them folded in such a way that their gleaming buttons showed, and unless being worn, our caps placed centrally overall.

At Uxbridge we had steel lockers on the wall above each bed and a wooden bed-side shelf/locker at the side of each bed. Normally our mugs and eating utensils were on the top shelf of this, with towel on a rail behind and our toilet gear on lower shelves. For a kit inspection, the mug stayed there but the K, N, and F, as they were soon known, were in the hold-all across the centre of the bed, together with razor, toothbrush, comb and the button-stick. The boots were, appropriately, at the foot end of the bed, upside down in all their gleaming glory.

In the steel locker were breeches, spare tunic, shirts, vests, PT kit and socks, all with tapes sewn onto them in conspicuous places - tapes about ¾ inch wide, with one's number printed on them of about equal size. This number, which had been given to us on enlistment, was unique to each and was a perfect means of identification. Used in Civvie Street, it could cause all kinds of heartburn among the ungodly and the ill-disposed.

Even our shoe-polishing brushes had to be spotless for inspections, and were expected to be cleaner than when issued, no traces of blacking or metal polish on them. Needless to say, we soon learned to duplicate as much of our kit as was affordable and obtainable, but that learning process, like most others, was hard and grim. There was a drawer within this steel locker which was more or less private and I suppose was meant for storing letters and writing materials etc., but items could be hidden behind folded kit if one were willing to take the risk - most were.

One thing must be said here, in view of stories one reads in newspapers of life in the modern services. In all the twelve years which I spent in the RAF, I cannot recall a single case of an airman being bullied, either by his comrades or by any NCO. Perhaps, what is these days considered as 'bullying', was then taken as just part of life in the Mob; certainly there were rough times had by all of us on occasion; times which didn't warrant the official designation of 'hard-lying' and thus to qualify the sufferer to an extra threepence per day.

What would perhaps be considered as bullying occurred during one of our periodic kit inspections. On arriving at the foot of my bed, the Sergeant-Major halted, and in a conversational tone of voice, asked, "Where's your razor, lad?" Because I did not yet shave, I replied, "I don't need one, Sir," and this brought the reply in rather a different tone of voice, "Well, show me your bloody emery-cloth!" Although not a little aghast at this at the time, the funny side took precedence over any other emotion soon afterwards.

My advice to latter-day soldiers is that if you can't take a joke you shouldn't have joined.

Although life did seem hard at times, and food not always to our liking, the RAF really did take an interest in our well-being; for instance, it was not left to us to see that we remained healthy, there were medical checks of every kind. A certificate of vaccination against smallpox had been a strict requirement before being accepted for enlistment, and when we were safely in the Mob there were inoculations against typhoid, bubonic plague and tetanus. This last was a regular three-monthly booster. Nothing was injected to prevent infection by what were then known as venereal diseases - except lectures on how to avoid them, and the information that these were regarded as self-inflicted injuries and the incapacity to perform one's RAF duties would result in loss of pay if nothing worse. I notice these days that V.D. has been promoted to S.T.D. or sexually transmitted disease; could that be because, since the invention or discovery of the sulpha drugs and penicillin, they are so little feared as to become standard.

Dental treatment was, like all other treatment - with the above exception - free, but with the proviso that a refusal of dental treatment could lead to one being no longer regarded as a dental responsibility. That may have been an 'old soldier's tale'- for I can't recall a single case of its occurring. My own first experience of service dentists nearly ended my RAF career almost before it had begun. Not more than a month after enlistment, it was discovered that I needed a filling. From a much later experience which I suffered, it may just have been that the dental officer felt like a little practice. However that may be, it is certainly true that many things were not so good in those far-off days as they are today, and dentists' drills are an example. When, during the drilling process, I suffered more than a little pain, I complained loudly: the dentist, being a Squadron Leader, took such umbrage at being called 'a cruel bastard' by a lowly recruit that he placed me on a charge. This was a new experience, but was not to be the last I fear. Coming up before the Group Captain - no less - several days later, I was asked by him if I liked life in the RAF, and if I did, I would be wise to temper my language when addressing an officer. Assuring him that I did indeed wish to remain in the RAF, he awarded me a mere three days C.B.

Among the various means the Service uses to make us fit to cope with what they might at any time want us to do, was a great deal of PT, and training in the RAF is certainly physical; not until the ripe old age of thirty-five could one expect to be excused PT. One event which took place as part of recruit training at Uxbridge was a boxing competition in which entry was not voluntary.

My little bout was going well until my opponent caught me one on the nose which was so painful that I applied to him the same epithet I'd used in the dentist's chair; but the consequences were not so drastic. I was merely disqualified!

One of the high spots of ANY week during this training period was the day on which the Golden Eagle defecated - pay day was the traditional one of Friday. This meant that one could now afford at least one good meal in the canteen; not that we were not fed adequately. We were, but not usually with the kind of food which a healthy young man fancies, viz., egg and chips or even sausages and ditto. Sunday morning breakfast was often a treat, when we were given bacon and egg, but with the active life we led, the appetite was seldom really satisfied.

Every morning there was a break between drill, PT, or other training sessions, when we rushed to the NAAFI for tea and a wad, always supposing that the necessary cash was to hand. It was during one of these welcome breaks that, standing in the queue, I overheard a fellow in the queue alongside mine mentioning the almost long-forgotten home town - Wolverhampton - of about three weeks ago!

This fellow and myself soon found out that our homes were only about a mile apart, and in the nature of 'fellow townies' we became friends although he was about a month senior to me, in both age and service; that doesn't sound much but at that time and place it was an eon. However, we remained close friends even when the 'exigencies of the Service' parted us, until his death in an aircraft accident in July 1941.

One incident which cemented our friendship was on the occasion, when returning from Christmas break at home, we were met at Paddington Station by his sister and a friend of hers. Before catching the Tube to Uxbridge, we repaired to a pub in Piccadilly called the Brasserie Universal. The last time I was in this pub it had changed its name to the White Bear; it's possibly some sort of night club these days if that corner of Regent Street allows such places.

We were having a very pleasant evening: the beer was good; there was a tzigane band of about six playing near to us at the bottom of the entrance stairway; and my pal Bert was so pleased with their performance that he was prompted to offer his packet of Player's cigarettes around. Unfortunately, their playing was better than their honesty, and the packet was returned in a nearly empty condition: this so annoyed Bert that he became a bit truculent, which brought the manager to our table. This poor fellow's remonstrances were ill-received by my pal, who, in the time-honoured manner of youth when it sees injustice and unfriendliness, hit him so hard that he slid across the polished floor. Without further ado, and not even saying toodle-oo to our companions, we grabbed our kit and were up those stairs and away, before reinforcements could arrive.

Just what his sister and her friend thought at the time I don't know, but I met her a long time afterwards and no recriminations were offered.

The final touch to this sorry story of youthful vandalism was that in negotiating the Piccadilly Underground Station, we both fell together down one of those long escalators and ended in an untidy heap at the bottom; and this, without physical damage to ourselves, but greatly to the detriment of my swagger cane, the beautiful silver knob of which was smashed flat!

CHAPTER 2
Grantham 3 F.T.S.

Because Bert had been in the RAF for a month longer than I, he, together with the rest of his squad, arrived at that long awaited time to pass-out from the Depot and go out into the greater and less hard world of the proper RAF; so sometime in January of 1935 off he went to No. 3 Flying Training School at Grantham, not that he had elected to go there - he had a girl at home so he probably asked for somewhere nearer home. I don't think Cosford was extant at that time, though doubtless it was on the cards. For reasons known only to the powers that be - but suspected by irks in general - when personnel were asked if they desired, or if they themselves requested, a posting to a station or unit near their homes it was always a sound bet that one would be posted as far away from there as would be possible without space travel!

However, when my turn came to pass out from basic training, I avoided anywhere near home and asked for RAF Grantham. I must have been the only one in the history of Uxbridge to get the posting asked for!

This was it then, the real Air Force, with aircraft flying around all day and the real possibility of an opportunity to fly in one. Somehow this didn't seem to be why I'd been sent there, having the low rank of Aircraftman second class in the trade of Aircrafthand. General duties didn't include dealing with real aeroplanes it seemed, and I was delegated to assist a corporal who was in charge of the three billiard tables in the canteen. This could be regarded as a sinecure perhaps, and I must admit that advantage was taken of an ideal situation in which to learn a new skill; a pity I've lost it in these days of high rewards for playing games!

My fellow new-boy, I found, had got himself a similar sinecure, if one in which he was more under the eye of authority: real authority in this case, for he was the Station Warrant Officer's runner, a gentleman whose service number was 52. He must have been in the RAF when Pontius was a Pilot and Jesus was a Corporal. Nonetheless, W.O. Cousins <u>was</u> a gentleman and that was not really a rare occurrence in the RAF; perhaps long service mellowed them.

It soon became apparent that Bertie had acquired himself a nickname with a modicum of derision in it. This friend of mine was the son of a First World War fighter pilot who had been killed in action when Bert was only eighteen months old. Like me, he had dreamed only of flying and aircraft since an early age: and had been unwise enough to voice his ambitions with the result that he was known to some of the less sympathetic souls as Sergeant-Pilot Jones; his subsequent service career would have shamed them had it been possible for them to foresee it. In the days before the mid-thirties the RAF - as also the other two Services - had been cut down considerably on the idea that Germany had been beaten and there was no one else who could bother us. Because of this, the total strength of the RAF was only thirty thousand, and they were spread over the world, keeping some sort of order, and this small force had a promotion rate which made it no place for the ambitious. To become a Sergeant Pilot one had first to be in a Group One trade, and to have a Group One trade, one needed to have been a Boy Entrant, or have been in since 1914 or thereabouts: in addition, one had to be a Leading Aircraftman at least, which entailed passing a test in your trade with at least 80% efficiency - after which pass, it usually took several years before a vacancy occurred at the same time as you were in good odour with your immediate superiors.

How then was HDB - known as hard-done-by Jones - going to make Sgt Pilot before retirement?

Just about that time, the penny was beginning to drop with the people who ran our country; boosted a little by a man named Beaverbrook who instigated the design and building of an aeroplane which was made by Bristol Aeroplane Co. Ltd., and known as Britain First, very similar to the later Blenheim of the early War years. All this stirred up the Government and they instigated what became known as the Expansion Programme - even this was helped along by the Daily Express when they enlisted one of their reporters, as No. 520163 - if I recall it correctly. This man's progress - daily - through the various trades and ranks of the service were a source of both amusement and not a little annoyance to the lads in grey-blue; but it certainly helped in the recruitment of new blood. Maybe the fact that the country was in a recession and jobs a bit hard to find had something to do with it too.

This new situation caused the RAF to look at what it had already, and there appeared a notice one day asking if any airman would like to be considered for remustering to Fitter, Aero-engine - we always describe things arse-about-face like that, it makes it easy for the store-keepers to change a hangar, aircraft to hanger, coat and sell it off cheap. However, HDB and myself put in for this and were given a local quizzing by the Station Engineer Officer, with surprisingly successful results in both our cases. Within what seems like no time in retrospect, we were on our way to where it had all started for us, West Drayton, and a trade-test board. We were there for three days and this was when our keenness about matters aeronautical brought dividends. There were some benefits in my own case from the priority given at school to metalwork instead of the maths which would have brought me into the RAF much quicker via Boy Entrance, but life is like that, a sort of balance sets up which compensates for apparent disadvantages.

There were one or two negative aspects to this success at West Drayton which disclosed themselves. Every year there occurred in the RAF an inter-station competition at Bisley; and by reason, I suppose, of my previous results in the Yeomanry, and of course, my young bright eyes, I was a fair shot and was selected for the station team at Bisley early in May. This was a very good "scrounge" for we spent every Thursday at Trent Bridge range near Nottingham, and buried large amounts of nickel-coated lead in the butts there. The results of the trade test at Drayton put paid to my continued participation in this pleasant occupation, for HDB and I were posted to No. 3 S. of T.T. at Manston on the 24th.

Every morning, on a Flying Training School in those far-off pre-war days, it was the usual practice that aircraft which were scheduled for training purposes on that day were flight tested for fifteen to thirty minutes, and this offered a good opportunity for such as we groundlings to see how the angels lived. Naturally, HDB and I had been taking as full advantage of this as was possible with the competition, and these trips in Avro Tutors and Hawker Harts would now be in the past.

Bert and I had also discovered that there was a gymnasium at Grantham which was fully equipped, even a full-size boxing ring; and enough fencing gear, canvas jackets, masks, gloves, foils, epees and sabres to kit out an army. All the time we were there, we two were the only people who used this gear as far as we knew.

It would be a pity to leave Grantham without one or two vignettes: one episode which lives in my mind was the parade through the town on the occasion of King George's Jubilee; George the Fifth that was, of course. Like most RAF camps, there was a station band at Grantham, and the drum major - the one who flings the mace around to give orders to his musicians both at rest and on the march - in this case was a corporal, a corpulent corporal at that. For this occasion I was one of those who were detailed to line the roads of the route. In those days we were there to mark out the route I think, so that we were allowed to turn our backs to the crowd and watch what was passing: in this rather less civilised age, route markers have to face the crowd to ensure that the multifarious nasties of this world can't take unrecorded and unobstructed pot-shots at the procession. This unfortunate corporal - major whilst performing one of the usually spectacular movements with his staff, loosed the thing and it sailed away in a parabolic trajectory to land among the crowd. Whilst I must admit that I found that just a bit amusing, the really remarkable aspect was that the crowd did not laugh, but there arose a kind of sigh which to me indicated sympathy rather than derision - and more credit to them.

One other little story I must tell, if it does go against myself. There was a young lady usher at the local cinema whom I rather fancied, and she occasionally let me take her home after the cinema closed. This was often followed by a little kiss and a cuddle before I had to be on my way up the two mile gradient to Spittlegate. One night she invited me to come to her home on the following Sunday for tea. Lovely! I thought, feet under the table. But it was not to be: certainly there was tea and home-baked cake, but there were also sundry queries about my prospects and even more startling, queries as to where I planned to live after we were wed! Needless to add, that this was the very last time I took her home or anywhere else; even the Luftwaffe didn't frighten me so much!

CHAPTER 3
Manston

When Bert Jones and I arrived at No. 3 School of Technical Training in the Isle of Thanet at Manston, it was a completely new world again for us. Without any doubt, that year we were to spend there was the 'tops' in modern parlance. Hard work there was in plenty, the first three months, for instance, were spent in learning the proper use of hand tools, such as the file, hacksaw, and the various measuring instruments.

Fitters we were going to be designated (if we passed), and fitters we were going to BE. The RAF possibly believes that an aircraft that is to fly first needs an aerodrome to take off from, or something like that. Anyway, I never met a pre-war fitter who couldn't file a piece of metal flat and level. Not that that was all we learned; there were lectures from real exponents of the art of keeping a kite flying, there was a good deal of practical work on real aero-engines such as the Bristol Jupiter and Napier Lion. Not least was the incessant note-taking and not just for our own edification, they had to be just about perfect, or else!

Some of the bright side of life at Manston was having both Margate and Ramsgate within two or three miles of the Camp, which made it seem like a long seaside holiday with interludes of work.

There was a regulation in force then that one had to have served for a minimum of one year before being allowed the privilege of wearing civvies, which was or seemed to us who were still practically rookies, to be unfair, with all the lads and lassies on the beaches etc., in summer gear. There was a little café in Ramsgate High Street and the proprietor kept a couple of rooms above it in which airmen could keep a suitcase containing their civilian gear and use it to change clothing before venturing forth into whatever adventure awaited one. It was expected that users of the facility also ate there, but he did a very good line in egg and chips so that was no hardship as long as the cash lasted. On one occasion, I was so much in a hurry to get to the Front that I failed to button up my flies and was strolling along with hands in pockets among the crowds of holiday-makers before noticing: in these days of tight jeans which tend to make young men look like ballet dancers it probably wouldn't be noticed, but in those more modest times I was aghast.

One of what may be called the disadvantages of Manston was the weekly church parade, which entailed the wearing of "Best Blue" viz. breeches and puttees; whereas at Grantham these parades had been possible to avoid for the most part, with the exception of a token presence to make the pupil pilots feel less put-upon.

To his credit, the Padre at Manston was something of a musical purist and liked his hymns to be sung with a vestige of the correct tune, and so formed a choir; which couldn't have been an easy matter with the material to hand!

However, when I discovered that the choir would proceed to the Camp church only in time to be there for the service - that is before the main parade personnel had finished their gyrations and gravel-bashing - and what was more to the point, that nicely pressed slacks would be the dress of the day, then I was a willing volunteer. There was a small price to pay; we needed to attend one practice evening in church, but the thirst engendered by such practices was soon assuaged with mugs of tea, brewed by the Padre on the large round coke stove which was used to heat the church hut.

There were two squadrons based at Manston then, which were of course, nothing to do with the training school except that they were all RAF. One day I was sent right across the aerodrome with a sackful of cleaning rags to Number Two Squadron, which at that time was equipped with Vickers Virginia bombers. It may seem laughable to the present-day reader to describe these gigantic box-kites as bombers, but to me then, they were beautiful because they flew, and the noise of those two Napier Lion engines was sweet music. I should have said sound rather than noise, but on this occasion of the rag-bag trip, it WAS noise; noise that suddenly awoke me to the fact that I was directly in the path of a Ginnie taking-off, and the bag over my shoulder had masked its presence: I just dropped flat on my face and hoped for the best - which happened.

Actually, the whole day was coloured by those cleaning rags. On arrival at the far side of the 'drome, 1 was pounced on by some NCO from 48 Squadron who needed some cheap labour, and who better than a poor defenceless young trainee from the School? I was given a tin of Brasso and some of the rags which I'd carried over and directed to a kite sitting on the tarmac. This was a Saro 'Cloud', an amphibian aircraft in which the twin engines were mounted on a sort of trellis-work amidships above the single mainplane.

"Just get those cowlings so I can see my face in 'em, and don't fall off the bloody wing," was the single definitive instruction I received.

He need have no qualms: to be actually working on a real aeroplane just made my day, although I must admit that in later years there were moments when such happy thoughts did not apply.

It was a nice sunny day, and clambering up onto the fuselage, and so to the wing centre section, I got well stuck into my polishing job on the engine cowlings. After about an hour of this, when the job was nearly finished and I was wondering what I could do to stretch out my expedition into the real RAF, a gentleman in a one-piece Sidcot suit strolled up, mounted the fuselage and dropped in through a hatchway just in front of the tail-unit. As he entered the aircraft he gestured me to come down and indicated that he intended to start the engines. So I gathered up my gear and moved smartly off the wing and sat on the back of the hatch with my feet dangling inside the fuselage.

It was quite pleasant sitting there with the engines blasting cool air at me after my polishing exertions, but the pleasure changed to slight panic when the Cloud began to taxi across the tarmac apron. It was too late to think of jumping off, so it was a case of fingers crossed. When the pilot - for such he was - proceeded to open up I realised that he intended taking off and I dropped quickly into the fuselage, where I moved up nervously to the cockpit.

There were no recriminations, just, "Sit down somewhere, and keep quiet," was all I got, so I did just that: and we had the nicest coastal trip up to the Thames estuary and back at about five hundred feet that I could have wished for, and not even a small rocket when we finally landed - luckily for me, at Manston.

In that first batch of trainees which had been filtered out from the RAF, there were only fifty-two of us and we were a mixed bunch of trades. Most of course, were aircrafthands, a generic term for those with no real trade. There was, I recall, a corporal Fabric-worker, who hailed from Walsall, but whose name eludes me, but he must have seen the light of the future, when aircraft would no longer be linen-covered frameworks (with apologies to that wonderful aeroplane, the Wellington).

Obviously this few bods was not going to be enough to allow a vast expansion of the Air Force; and as the weeks rolled on we found that the later intakes of trainees were coming more or less straight from Civvie Street.

There were many good engineering workers who had become redundant to the ship building industry in those depression days of the thirties; and most of them had spent seven-year apprenticeships to gain their skills - who better for the RAF to take on and make use of these skills?

One consequence of the influx was that we had to relearn English from a North Country aspect. Many things I learned in the Service, one of which was that when people of different local or national dialects live and work together, they soon acquire a sort of lingua-franca that will, over the course of time, almost obliterate their own local accents. Add to that the technical and foreign phrases abounding in Service conversation and we have a language which is pure RAF.

Few of us had vehicles, and even bicycles were rare; I bought a push-bike from a shop in Ramsgate, but most of the hire-purchase payments were paid by my mother. One lad did buy an Ariel Red Hunter which was the envy of most of us, certainly of myself. He arrived in that happy state by means of hard work and some luck: his folk owned a sweet and tobacco shop, and supplied him with stock which he then flogged to us paupers on 'tick'; usually by about Wednesday, if not before, we were stony broke and it was easy to say, "Give us ten fags till Friday," or to buy a bar of Cadbury's if one hadn't the price of a tea and a wad in the NAAFI. One must add that the prices he charged were the same that similar items would have cost in the canteen; but his folks must have had an excellent turnover.

There was one fellow who lent actual money, AND charged interest, but then, HIS father was a vicar, and so perhaps he was only trying to teach us to be more careful!

There was one other fellow with a motorcycle, whose machine was a BSA with a large side-car attached. On one memorable night he brought seven of us back to camp from an evening in Margate with this outfit. I was on the back end of the chair with my feet and lower legs trapped by the two bods sitting in the chair; and with the seat of my breeches not many inches from the nasty rough road surface. Even at that I consider that I was better off than the two standing on the unsprung connection tubing.

But these adventures were only brief interludes in the process of our learning to become useful members of the RAF. By the very fact of the now recognised need to expand our forces, it was going to be a more condensed and concentrated course of instruction than the erstwhile Boy-Entrant one.

This had been quite efficient and perfect for the Air Force of the twenties and early thirties, when numbers were not considered to be essential.

A peace-time force is always thought of as just another one of those overheads which the country could well do without. At Halton, boys were accepted by means of selective and competitive examinations from the age of 15¾ to 17½; and in addition to the necessary technical instruction, they were given a good general education which was about the equivalent of that obtainable at a minor public school. Most of them took complete advantage of this: I met a sergeant fitter in France who held a B.Sc., Eng. and he couldn't have been more than twenty-six years old.

Apart from the day-to-day marching from our huts to the workshops and back, the main excitements - if such they can be called - were our trips into either Ramsgate or Margate. The latter had a sort of Disneyland which went under the unlikely name of Dreamland which attracted the youth of London, and so, some of us! Ramsgate was a more sedate venue, except perhaps in winter, when there was All-In Wrestling on - of all times - Sunday evenings. The wrestling had a rival attraction on windy nights, when the sea would often batter against the promenade wall and create havoc with the polish of our greatcoat buttons!

One day in high summer we were invited to enter a team in a Pushball league. This game consisted of opposing teams pushing a giant eight foot diameter ball on a course marked out on the beach. Those of us in my team ended the day with most of the skin off our bodies from sand abrasion, and our lungs full of seawater because of our poor performance, but it was good publicity for the RAF.

All things come to an end, and the time came for the examination and testing of our newly acquired skills and knowledge. There was naturally a test of our skill with file and micrometer, which consisted of producing an amazingly useless object. When finished, it consisted of ¼ inch steel plate exactly two inches square, in two pieces, one of which was in the form of the letter Y with the foot and two upper arms terminating in ½ inch square parts, each of which could be fitted into the female part of the whole, and in any way the examiner chose - without any light showing between the mating parts.

Sounds terribly difficult to me even now after all these years - and so it was! Not so difficult, however, as I found one of the practice pieces during our course. This was also based upon a two inch square of steel plate, but with a one inch square hole centrally placed. Into this aperture had to be fitted a cube of Duralumin in every which-way. The Dural, incidentally, was cut from damaged Fairey Reed metal airscrews, and I must have reduced at least one airscrew blade to filings in the process of forming my cube. The great difficulty was that, just as the piece was coming down to size, the use of a very fine file to obtain the required finish caused swarf to build up between the teeth of the file, which cut a series of grooves across the surface! Attempts to file out the groove resulted in an undersized piece and a fresh start.

Nonetheless, when the results of our exams were promulgated, I found that I was considered to be 66% efficient, which had the happy result of my passing out as Aircraftman First Class in the Group One trade of Fitter, Aero-engine: a proud moment, and the pleasure was increased because my pal HDB had done equally well.

The Fabric-worker corporal actually passed out with over 80% marks, and against all the accepted air force folk-lore we'd had, became a leading aircraftman.

Now both Bert and myself were on the way to 'sergeant pilot' and that coveted brevet over the left tunic pocket.

CHAPTER 4
Thornaby

Where we should be posted now became the subject of conversation; in accordance with RAF tradition one had to suggest a unit which was stationed as far away from where one actually desired to go if one was to stand any chance of getting there. This was a process very similar to backing zero at roulette. Having this foreknowledge of failure, both Bert Jones and I left it to the RAF and the luck of the draw; with the result that he was posted to RAF Digby in Lincolnshire, which was inhabited by a Flying Training School; and I was posted to Thornaby-on-Tees, another FTS, which I always thought was No. 10, but which a copy of my Service documents tells me was in fact No 9. It seems that I didn't know what Unit I belonged to for over a year: no wonder that I never made Group Captain!

Well, never mind what the Unit's number was; after a short leave, from which I proceeded directly to Thornaby, I became at last a useful member of the RAF, or so I liked to think.

We had several types of kite there: there were, of course, what was the usual dual-control two-seater trainer, the Avro Tutor together with Hawker Harts, Audaxes and Demons for more advanced training; some of which were dual-control. We even had one or two Hawker Furies, single-seater fighters, which were beautiful, delicate little aircraft. At Grantham there had also been examples of the forerunner to the Tutor - the Avro 504 N, with the same Armstrong-Sidderley engine as its successor: the rotary engined 504 K was a bit before my time, but doubtless examples were still flying around in India and the Middle East.

Life became far more hectic now; there never seemed enough hours in the day for what we had to do. Although but a newly trained fitter, I was allocated a Hart all to myself - enginewise - and the day started with the daily inspection of this lovely black-enamelled Kestrel 1B. Inspection was the right word, it meant looking at every part with a discerning eye; it also covered checking the state of the oil and coolant, of ensuring a full fuel tank, and of test-running the engine. This last with the aid of someone to wind the starting-handle; then of checking both magnetos and the condition of the sparkplugs (by switching each mag off separately and noting the drop in engine revolutions); and generally making damn sure that nothing was likely to fall off the aeroplane when in the air.

One of the perquisites of being on an F.T.S. was that the pupils, most of whom were Acting Pilot Officers, were generally obliged to help in the general maintenance and cleanliness of the aircraft. They had to carry out menial jobs, such as the polishing of engine cowlings, which were of aluminium sheeting; whereas the wings and fuselage of the Hawkers and Avros were fabric-covered and finished with silver-coloured dope. They also did most of the manual work entailed in swinging the compasses. This involved moving the aeroplane around on a special concreted area, the surface of which was marked out clearly with the points of the compass. As the kite was revolved over this area to be lined up with the points, the reading of the inboard compass was checked for co-incidence, and adjusted accordingly by moving small magnets around its casing if necessary.

Naturally, ground crews took some pleasure in the reversal of normal roles in this way, but isn't this always so; underlings often like to take advantage when in unaccustomed positions of authority, but it must be added that no real animosity was ever shown or developed by this ruling.

One exception I should mention, even though it does perhaps reflect little credit on the writer.

One day, as a new intake of pupils was marching along the tarmac to one of the lecture rooms, I recognised one of them as a lad who had been at school with me in the same class. I waved to him and sought him out after their dismissal, but he pretended not to know me and ignored my advances. I must admit that I was a bit dumbfounded and not at all pleased; so I made no further attempt to renew acquaintance. I found later that he was posted to a bomber squadron equipped with Handley-Page Hampdens; and he was involved in one of the first air-raids on the Kiel Canal with this squadron; unfortunately for him his aircraft was shot down and he and his crew spent the war years as prisoners. And sad to state, this caused me a little pleasure...

Even as early as 1936, there were obvious signs that the Government was becoming seriously engaged in strengthening our Air Force. When I arrived at Thornaby, we were using those Bessoneau hangars which were used in France during the Great War (1914-18), but there were new brick-built ones in the process of being erected, with steel doors fixed with ballast so that each weighed around ten tons, and with side offices for crew rooms and stores.

A real glimpse of the future one day, was the arrival of a visitor. This was an Osprey, one of the Hawker group of aircraft designed for use by the Fleet Air Arm, with arrestor gear for deck landings and mop for deck swabbing. This aeroplane was painted in a drab mixture of green and brown, which made it stand out among our silver Harts and yellow Tutors.

The flying course of the pupils was designed to fit them for service with an active squadron, and included cross-country flights to other stations, and of course those raisons d'être of an air force, air-gunnery and bombing practices. Some of this last was carried out at Thornaby using the camera obscura principle. There was a square building at the far side of the 'drome which had one door, no window, and a small hole in the roof. Underneath this hole a table was sited with a map of the area, on which was marked the position of the camera obscura hut. When an aircraft flew overhead within range, a small image of it passed across the map. The aircraft was equipped with a container with a number of magnesium photoflash bulbs which could be fired individually by the aircrew. When this was done the flash of the bulb was shown up quite visibly on the map in the hut and a judgement made about the accuracy of the 'bombing'; cheap, and very fascinating to a young airman.

For more violent and spectacular practising, the unit migrated to one or other of the RAF's Practice Camps, either North Coates Fitties in Lincs., or Catfoss in Yorkshire. It was to Catfoss that we went in February of 1937, a bleak place to spend much time in, with those oh so bracing winds off the North Sea. However, there were compensations. It was there that I saw my first Gauntlet, and fell in love with it and its successor, the Gladiator; one day, a Westland Wallace dropped in for refuelling. I've a lovely fossil ammonite still, which is a souvenir of that Wallace - it spanged up from under its tyre whilst I was assisting the pilot to taxi off the tarmac apron - and hit me right in the groin.

For bombing practice, there was a wooden float job, painted yellow for visibility which was towed out to sea by an RAF launch. The idea was not to hit it and sink it, but to aim off a number of degrees, which could give an idea of the accuracy of the aim. The bombs used were 9½ lb practice bombs with a cast iron body in which moved the firing pin, and a sheet-steel finned tail unit which contained stannic chloride in liquid form. When the firing pin struck the detonator within the tailpiece the SnCl was scattered and formed a dense white cloud which looked quite fearsome. Not that the things were completely harmless, a nine pound lump of cast iron would just about sink the towing launch with a direct hit.

The aeroplane which was my particular responsibility whilst at Catfoss was a Hawker Hart, one which was fitted with a Kestrel engine actually made at Derby by Rolls Royce themselves. That may sound peculiarly naive, but when one compared such an engine with another which had been built in what were known as shadow factories - these were factories under the auspices of Morris Motors - there was a very noticeable difference. Certainly they looked alike and there was only a slight difference in their performances, but the engine in my Hart ran as sweet as a sewing machine, with not a vestige of vibration, even when run up to maximum T/O revs; and she was the apple of my eye.

Whilst at Catfoss, it was customary to run a weather flight to ascertain visibility, and this was flown fairly early in the day, before any other flight; in fact before breakfast. The procedure was for the kite to ascend to about ten thousand feet, and then to descend in stages of one thousand feet. At each altitude, the pilot fired a Very light of a pre-arranged colour or combination of colours. The lights were cartridges similar to 12 bore shotgun ammo, but much larger - about two inches in diameter by three inches long - and fired from a fearsome looking weapon known, of course, as a Very pistol. Although when used from an aircraft it was clipped into a tube fixed to the cockpit floor, which, one presumes, obviated any chance of the firework coming into contact with any part of the aircraft.

The motor launch which was used to tow the target float would be cruising around in the target area and record which of the Very colours he could distinguish clearly and thus arrive at the bombing altitude at which there would be least chance of the launch being mistaken for the target float!

For one of these early morning test-flights my Hart was detailed. The pilot must have been in a great hurry for his breakfast that morning, because he finished his visibility checks at about five thousand feet and just put the kite into a powered dive to land almost out of the dive. The effect on that Kestrel was devastating; when I checked it over for later flights, I found several small leaks of glycol from the external coolant joints, and the engine never ever ran smoothly whatever I tried. I came to the conclusion that she must have been over the top in revs and the cylinder blocks had expanded to a point when permanent distortion had occurred.

It was whilst we were at Catfoss that we lost one of our Furies. An instructor who lived in Ireland took the Fury for a flight to Aldergrove, and managed to find the seaward face of the Mourne Mountains in poor visibility, with fatal consequences to both of them.

Furies didn't seem to have a great survival record with this FTS. One of them crashed in the Cleveland Hills to the south of Thornaby. The pilot mistook a bog area for nice smooth turf and wrecked the kite, but not himself happily. The salvage crew who went out to see what could be brought back, removed the engine and placed it on a sheet of corrugated iron to tow it onto harder ground; unfortunately, they found that the Morris six-wheeler they had with them was, itself, sunk into the bog to the axles; and immovable.

Frantic calls for help brought the Army with a Bren-carrier tracked-vehicle. Sad to relate, however, the weather wasn't helping much and the carrier became another casualty. Not to be beaten, a tank transporter was brought along and securely anchored on solid ground several hundred yards away, and the two bogged-down vehicles plus our unfortunate Kestrel from the Fury, were towed ignominiously onto firmer ground, with the winch and cable.

Strangely enough, it was another Fury's misfortune that occurred later in the history of this FTS. We had moved to Hullavington in Wiltshire, of which more later, and the request came to us to collect a Fury from one of the fighter squadrons which had force-landed some miles away. For this expedition we again used that old work-horse, the Morris six-wheeler; the plan here was to remove the mainplanes and tow the fuselage home with the tail-skid in the back of the truck and its own wheels on the road.

This sounds fairly straightforward, but there were snags. The first snag was that there was quite a lot of work entailed in removing the mainplanes, and by the time this was accomplished we were a little displeased with the pilot who had landed in a field which was too damn small to take off from. When this task ended, it was decided to take the fuselage to camp first, and return for the wings later. The tail was lifted into the back of the Morris and the tail-skid fitted into a sort of box nailed to the floor, so that the aircraft pivoted about its tail. Because the wheel bearings of the Fury were plain phosphor-bronze, it was going to be necessary to stop quite often en route to grease these bearings as they were not really designed for continuous use over public roads. However, everything went swimmingly until we were within a couple of miles of home, when we came to a T-junction where we needed to turn quite sharply to the left onto a major road. Major roads then of course, were just rather more important ones than country lanes, not the six-lane jobs we think of nowadays. Up until now it had rather more gentle turns, but this was a bit tight; thinking nothing of it, the driver turned left. There was a very nasty sound from the Fury as its port longerons came into devastating contact with the side of the Morris, and when we saw the reason - a nice serviceable fuselage with a pronounced kink where it should be straight - there was much distress and gnashing of teeth; why we were not all shot on our return to Hullavington, I'll never understand.

Things happen like that in the RAF; when you think you're for the high jump, nothing happens, but the reverse is more often. One thinks, "That was a good job, chiefy will be pleased with me," but find that there is a considerable rocket coming your way instead; it's almost like being married.

There used to be a pub in Stockton which held sing-songs which provided instrumentalists on Sunday nights (great venue for us young lads to get rid of high spirits), but it was quite organised. If anyone wished to get on his hind feet and 'carol' forth there was usually a request for 'a bit of ush'. On the other side of Stockton's very wide main street, there was a pub called The Vane Arms, the kind of pub which is very popular these days, half-timbered and low ceilings etc. This was a pub with the reputation of being a good place to pick up the girls, and so it was, but not the sort of girl which may spring to the mind of the reader. No, I personally always found them to be reasonably respectable types, it was just that it wasn't the accepted thing in those days for girls to go into pubs. Stockton girls were a law unto themselves however. Some years ago now, I was in the north of England and bethought myself, "I'll have a pint in the Vane," but it was hard luck, they'd knocked it down and built a shopping centre on the site. My nostalgic ardour received a further blow when I drove past where I thought RAF Thornaby was and found a housing estate there; it was only the remaining presence of one of the old hangars which saved me from thinking I was going round the bend. It really is remarkable just how many of those old war-time and pre-war aerodromes have been appropriated for housing the vastly increased populace; or is it that everyone seems to want a house to themselves these days?

And speaking of housing estates and Thornaby reminds me of a story about what was known as 'married-patch' there.

From time to time various duties were allotted to us, such as guard duties and fire-pickets. This last usually meant only that one was confined to camp bounds for the period of the duty - mostly twenty-four hours - and in the event of a fire alarm, to report for duty to the fire-fighting section. There was one exception; each tour of duty always included one aircraft or MT fitter who reported himself to the booster unit. This was a water pump unit driven by a petrol engine which increased water pressure in the system connected to the fire hydrants from that of normal mains pressure. A further task was to ensure that the valves controlling the supply to the hydrants were correctly open, and that the normal usage system was isolated. This really was asking for it; and sure enough, on one momentous occasion, the pump engine was started up and the valves not changed over - with the expected shocking results in the kitchens, bathrooms and toilets of the married quarters!

Night flying was an important part of the flying courses, and usually went off quite harmlessly except for ground crew being frozen stiff for the duration of operations. There was one never-to-be-forgotten night when an aircraft, after taking off apparently well, failed to gain height and crashed into a small woodland just beyond the airfield. There was not a great deal left of either aircraft or pilot as a result, and a lead-lined coffin was needed. The sequel to this tragedy was that, because the lad's parents wished for him to be buried near home, six of us were detailed to act as bearers and guard of honour to carry his coffin to the railway station. All went well en route; the six of us sitting alongside the coffin in the back of the faithful Morris six-wheeler, lowering him gently down outside the station, draping the RAF Ensign over him and placing his service cap on top. Then, a steady slow march onto the platform to the waiting train; all very impressive and solemn. Bathos and chaos from hereon;

and the first misfortune was that we had to load him into a goods van which had been specially added to the train. It was obviously not very practical to have put the fellow's coffin into a normal passenger compartment, apart from the difficulty of easy access with such an object; but underlining the dismay we bearers felt was the fact that written in white chalk in quite large lettering right across the damned side of this goods van were the words "Pigeons Only!"

Our NCO slid open the doors of the van, we proceeded to move aboard, and it was at this point that disaster really struck. The floor of the van was about two feet above the platform level and the two front bearers stepped up into the van with the coffin still on their shoulders without thinking of lowering it and sliding it along the floor. We at the rear were taken a bit by surprise by this sudden elevation to an angle of forty-five degrees and couldn't lift the rear sufficiently quickly or high enough to prevent cap and Ensign from sliding ignominiously to the platform.

All in all, we were glad to slide the van doors shut and sneak out of the station in shame.

It may have been this episode, or a collection of others, but soon afterwards there were rumours that the School was moving to a new location in Wiltshire, where - as we found - none of the locals had yet met the RAF; but one further epic accident must be recounted. The design of the Hawkers was such that care needed to be taken when taxiing or landing to use the Palmer pneumatic brakes gently. The centre of gravity of these aeroplanes being rather forward, they tended to tip onto the nose fairly easily, which was not too good for the airscrew. It was not an uncommon sight to see a Hart or an Audax with its tail in the air and its pilot with his tail between his legs. Because one never knows what to expect with air accidents, the ambulance and fire engine always made quick time to the scene; and this was the case on this occasion. Unfortunately, when the ambulance, in this case an old plywood-sided vehicle, was half way across the 'drome to where the offending kite was on its nose, another aircraft was taking off on an intersecting course. They met when the Audax was about six feet into the air with the result that it rose vertically above, somersaulted over the ambulance, landing some sixty or so feet in front of it and upside down. Luckily, the sick-bay wallah had been sitting nonchalantly in the rear doorway, and had the presence of mind to drop off before the impact, but the crew of the kite, pupil and instructor, were trapped in their cockpits. The one in the observer's, or rear seat, looked in a bad way, but the driver was quite eloquent. With a strong smell of 87 octane around and little fingers of flame around the engine area, we had to work pretty fast. I still bear a scar on the palm of my hand from a broken flying wire as we tried to drag the broken wing away and lift the fuselage enough to get them both out. We did; but we, and they, were soaked in foam from the fire-engine crew's efforts to save us from a sticky end.

CHAPTER 5
Hullavington

The rumours of our impending move to our new base in Wiltshire were confirmed in the first week of July '37, when about a dozen of us, with assorted trades and ranks, were detailed as an advance-party. By the eighth we were cleared from Thornaby and on our way.

Getting 'cleared' was usually quite a bore and almost the last thing one did on a unit. When 'posted' i.e. allotted to another unit, personnel were given a 'clearance chit', which was essentially a list of all the departments or sections of a unit which might have a claim on them, such as borrowed tools, barrack damages liability, monies owed for clothing issue; anything in fact for which no further action could be taken without a great deal of bother once one was away. The whole process could take days before every section on one's list had given clearance; including being paid up to date. When being posted solo as it were, there was also the issue of movement orders and railway warrants where applicable, but in the instance of our movement to Wiltshire the NCO i/c took care of this aspect; and because we were not actually leaving No.10 FTS, our clearance chits were not absolute.

The day came when all were clear, and it only remained for us to draw our packed lunches - which were officially known as 'the unexpired portion of the day's rations' - and we were away.

We took the local train from Stockton to Darlington - that historic line - with no trouble, and there we piled all our kit on one of those flat platform trucks which were usually available. Seldom are these unwieldy vehicles to be seen nowadays - nor the porters who used them for moving mailbags and all the parcels and packages which used to litter the platforms. In these less honest, or more openly dishonest, days the trolleys used for platform transport have cages built into them to protect their loads, but at least one can't trip over them so easily.

Our idea was to have everything ready when our train for King's Cross came in from Scotland. We were not to know that the train was late - and this in an era when this mattered to train-crews - and that the driver would be impatient to be on his way. Certainly, it seemed that the train had hardly stopped long enough for passengers who wished to alight, when it began to move again. There were porters with mail etc., to load into the guard's van. Luckily Darlington had a long platform and it was a long train; but we only just managed to throw everything on to the train and then pile into the van ourselves before the speed increased, had it been a modern electric loco, we should never have made it. The last thing I saw of Darlington Station was that platform truck careering down the slope at the end of the platform; God knows where it ended up!

Nothing very memorable occurs to me about the journey to London or the transfer to Paddington by Underground, so we must have behaved ourselves fairly well. We must have changed trains at Swindon for a local train, which eventually carried us to a small station near our new camp destination, Hullavington.

Here we met with a brand new RAF Station, which had - we were told by the contractors - been two years in the building and was not yet quite finished.

The aerodrome itself was of grass, as most 'dromes were at that time, but this one at Hullavington could have been used as a substitute venue for the Wimbledon Tennis Championships. It was so perfectly conditioned and flat. Most of the airfields of the RAF in pre-war days could be relied upon to grow a good crop of mushrooms in the season; it was thought that plentiful bullshit was the main reason, but that's perhaps unsubstantiated - fungi were absent from Hullavington, as indeed, were weeds.

The hangars, of which there were several, were built of that almost pure white freestone known as Bath stone, with the exception, of course, of the ten-ton doors which were the new steel bomb-proof ones. They were reputed to be bomb-proof because the steel frame was filled with ballast, and their weight made it necessary to move them by means of cranked handles to revolve the wheels upon which they moved.

All of the buildings on this camp were of the same beautiful stone; the four barrackblocks, the canteen, senior NCOs' Mess and the Officers' Mess; even the central heating boiler house and water tower were white. When I say central heating, it was just that, one boiler house from which a glass-fibre insulated pipeline fed all buildings. This was still being installed when we, the advance party, arrived, so we didn't get the full advantage of it; at least it was still summer, and that summer of 1937 was quite a good one.

There was not a great deal of work for us to do, with no aircraft yet arriving, apart perhaps from that salvage job on the Fury, of which the least said the better.

There were, however two very interesting towns both of which were within five miles of the camp. Malmesbury, with its abbey and old buildings; and the market town of Chippenham, with its pubs.

One of our party, an LAC named Mitchell, had only recently returned from a five-year term in India, and was desirous of finding somewhere to live off the camp so that he could bring his wife down from Northumberland and this gave us a useful undertaking. Another of the group was a Cpl Armourer whom I can only remember as Jackie. The three of us spent some time scouring the vicinity for suitable digs for Mitch. One evening, we ended up in a small village about three miles from camp called Grittleton, and popped into the local pub, The Red Lion then, to further our enquiries and slake our thirsts. This was about the best thing we did at Hullavington. Mitch found a fellow there who was willing to take him and his wife in, at least for a few weeks until he could fix more permanent quarters via the RAF. Not only that, but he invited the three of us to supper at his house in the village, and this became an almost regular event. This gentleman was a gardener working for the local squire, who was a fanatical grower of orchids, and also interested in the village cricket team. It so happened that Grittleton was rather short of cricket-playing-age manpower that summer, and all three of us were invited to join the team; incidentally we also became members of the pub darts team. By reason of what were called 'the exigencies of the Service', I only played in one away and one home match with the cricket team, but they were both very enjoyable. Some years ago, before the M4 was built so near to Grittleton that the air there must now be polluted, I called at the pub and found that the name had been changed from The Red Lion to the something Arms, a name which eludes me, but was the name of that local squire who was so fond of orchids and who must have been well thought of in the village.

The reason why I had to give up this idyllic life in the heart of England's cricketing country was another posting, this time to the Fleet Air Arm.

By coincidence, HDB Jones, whom I had first met at the Uxbridge Depot, had more or less followed a similar career to my own. When

I'd been posted to Thornaby, he'd gone to RAF Digby, which was also a Flying Training School. Whilst there a posting had come through for him to Bermuda; and of all places it was possible for an erk to be sent, that was like winning the Irish Sweep. But Bert was engaged to a girl from home and wasn't as pleased as he should have been. In some interesting way which I was never privy to, he could cause his tonsils to inflame, and found this quite useful when he wanted to avoid an unpleasant duty like, say, fire-picket at the weekend. Well, he pulled this one for the Bermuda posting, and it worked, to his and his girlfriend's delight.

Someone once said that, "You can buck the corporal, buck the sergeant; even buck the group captain, but you can never buck the Air Force". HDB found the truth of this just before my posting to the Fleet Air Arm came through when his posting to HMS Glorious dropped out of the blue. This time when he went sick with tonsillitis, the RAF whipped him into hospital and severed his chances of ever pulling that one again.

And now it was my turn, with a posting to HMS FURIOUS, an aircraft carrier then lying at Devonport. This was an urgent posting apparently; I had a quick visit to a civilian dentist in Chippenham, a quick whip around the camp with a clearance chit and I was off - to sea.

CHAPTER 6
Furious

It had been an interesting journey through a part of England which I had not seen before. From Malmesbury, I'd travelled through late summer-sun-drenched Wiltshire to Bristol, Temple Meads; and from there, right across beautiful moorland areas, over viaducts, along river valleys; to drop down into Plymouth in late evening, just as dusk fell.

Picking up my kitbag and the old leather suitcase with my civvies and a few books inside, I staggered out of the carriage onto the platform and wondered what my next step would be. I needn't have worried, after all, I was in the RAF and it always looks after its own even if it doesn't always appear to do so.

But it was no RAF bod who called out to me, "You for FURIOUS?" It was a Naval petty officer.

"Yes," I responded.

"I've got a gharry outside for you; that your kit?" and with that he picked up my kitbag and led the way out of the station.

"No check at the ticket gate - a PO chauffeur! They must think I'm their new Captain in disguise," I mused.

Settled in beside the driver in the cab of his pickup, with my kit flung carelessly into the open back, we drove along strange streets, some of which showed railway lines along them - most peculiar - we eventually arrived in one deserted stretch of road with building on either side.

"Here you are then," said my new friend. "Out you get."

"Where's the ship, then?" I asked, seeing nothing that looked even faintly like one to me.

"That's her, behind you," he replied, pointing over my shoulder. "The gangway is just down there, where the light is."

Turning round, all I could see was a slab of wall about twenty feet high, which seemed to extend for miles in either direction; but I could see the gangway, and when I got used to the idea I could see that the wall was indeed a ship.

Climbing that gangway, I was greeted first by a marine sentry who directed me along a narrow deck towards the 'front end' - later to be known as 'up forrad' - where I should find some RAF types. It now appeared that I was lucky in one way, for I was joining the ship half-way through a 'cruise'. In those days, crews of naval vessels were changed completely at intervals of about two years, a practice which no doubt was started in the days of Nelson, when two years was about a lifetime in wooden ships.

It transpired that one of the present complement of RAF aero-engine fitters had been taken so ill that he had either been posted away or had died; I never really found out what had happened to him and suspected that my new shipmates were being kind to me - that is partly what I meant by being lucky, everyone else had been aboard for some months and were generally willing to help the new boy. About a year later, I was able to return this help to a completely fresh lot of 'green' erks - and shoot a bit of a line at the same time - because when the ship's crew changed, and with it the RAF contingent, I was left to soldier on with the new postings; not that, at the time it was very obvious that I was an old sea-dog because we were all ashore at RAF Gosport when the ship re-commissioned: but more of Gosport later.

Moving up forward as instructed, I was met by a lad from the Orderly Room, who noted my movement orders and checked me in as it were. He then took me along to what he called the E.R.S. or engine repair shop, but which to me seemed rather like a small office with doors which weighed several hundredweight each. In the corner of this workshop was a smaller office which was not only the E.R.S. stores, but also the private domain of the Senior N.C.O. i/c E.R.S.; his office, his bedroom or bunk and probably his bathroom! The whole of this workshop and stores probably extended to an area of about twenty-five feet by twelve feet.

Having greeted me, this sergeant showed me to my quarters; this turned out to be a small corner of the workshop, with a cupboard area underneath a workbench which was really intended for tool storage, and a couple of hooks which some past inhabitant had fixed to the bulkheads for hammock slinging. Some slight elucidation needed here perhaps; bulkheads are what landlubbers call walls, and a hammock is a canvas sheet with multiple eyelets along the ends to which are tied strings called clews which in turn are tied to a metal ring, which also receives a rope for attaching the hammock to suitable fixings. Just how one was supposed to get into this I'll leave to the reader's imagination. There were also two very good quality white woollen blankets. When not in use for sleeping in or falling out of, the whole caboodle had to be rolled up tightly and the slinging ropes used to lash it neatly, using, if I recall correctly, seven turns around the circumference and finishing with one along the length through each of the seven lashings. This, of course, was a marvellous object for lining the bulwarks of Nelson's ships to keep musket balls and cannon ditto from wreaking their intended havoc; and they were very useful when the ship sank because, it was said, they would float for a long time.

I had no need for either of these uses, but I certainly found it a much better place for sleeping than the top of a workbench, when, later, the 'old flat-top' was at sea and the water wouldn't keep still.

The first priority on joining any new RAF unit was always to find what we called a 'bed-space', that small patch of the world's surface which an erk could call his own. No such area existed in the Navy, not on board ship anyway, every available space had a positive naval usage, which personnel may possibly be permitted to occupy part-time. So, I suppose I'd been doubly lucky in taking over from someone who had managed to allocate to himself a small piece of this damn great ship: I was to do even better for myself later.

There was a pair of double watertight doors in the aft bulkhead of our E.R.S. workshop which led into a short - eight feet or so - airlock area with a further pair of similar doors at the aft end, dividing it from a large area of the lower aircraft hangar lying forward of the forward lift-well. If this seems unduly complicated, that may be because it takes some time to find one's way readily around a large naval vessel. Anyway, to cut a long story short, I managed to arrange matters so that I could swing my hammock between the two pairs of doors of this airlock passageway, making sure that the overlapping door of each pair was shut first; suffocation was not on my agenda. For when we were not at sea, I managed to obtain a folding camp-bed to erect in my secure little cabin.

Above the workshop was an area called the mess-deck, where all forty-eight members of HQ Flight ate, and where many of them slung hammocks or slept on the tables according to personal choice, if the word choice applies here.

At that time the 'Command' units of the Fleet Air Arm were all manned by RAF personnel and were known as Flights; in the case of FURIOUS the total complement was one Flight of Hawker Ospreys, a two-seater fighter/reconnaissance aircraft which was another of those very versatile derivatives of the Hart, powered by a super-charged Rolls Kestrel of 640 h.p., and two Flights of Fairey Swordfish with Bristol Pegasus 9 cyl. radials. The Ospreys belonged to 801 Flight and the two Flights of Swordfish to 821 and 822. 821 Flight had only recently been re-equipped from having Blackburn Sharks, an earlier type of torpedo bomber, and one which I have never even seen.

Nowadays, and possibly during the last war, flights in the FAA are called squadrons, as the equivalent strength unit is called in the RAF; but to all intents and purposes the operational Flights were Squadrons, with their own maintenance and flying crews. By the time I joined ship, many of the aircrew were already matelots, but it so happened that I myself was the first of what one must call 'ground staff', to be relieved by a Naval aircraft artificer in FURIOUS at least, and that was in January of 1939.

For major work on aircraft, such as 120 hour inspections and engine changes, we of HQ Flight were carried. These four dozen bods also undertook general administration tasks for the whole RAF contingent and apart from engine fitters and airframe riggers, there was at least one fabric-worker, there was a corporal Coppersmith, Jack Oyler, who hailed from the Scillies, and his blacksmith/welder mate, there were Clerks for the Orderly Room and the Pay dept., and a number of Storekeepers.

Cooks, and most of the disciplinary matters were taken care of - well and truly - by the Navy. Thoughts of cooks bring to mind that the grub in this ship at least, was much better than that which we had in the RAF. When one remembers that in the early thirties our generous Government allowed only 9d per day each to feed everyone in the Service, and then consider how that princely sum would be allocated between officers, N.C.O.'s and men, it was much to the credit of our cooks that we were generally fairly well, and well fed.

After a few years in the RAF, one soon became used to changes of scene and the new faces which surrounded one; in fact it was always probable that at least one of the bods on one's new station - or ship, in this case - would be someone whom you had met before. In this event it was often the case that you became friends, partly because of shared memories I suppose, however fleeting one's previous acquaintance had been.

Not this time however; having been in the RAF for only three years at this time, and most of my new shipmates being real old soldiers, I had not met any of them previously. Old salts would perhaps be a more fitting description. It was usual for RAF Records to post personnel to the FAA who had already served one cruise either in a carrier or in one of those cruisers which carried a seaplane; the indisputable reason was that overseas postings to India, the Middle East, the China Station, Malaya and Singapore, etc., were of five years' duration, and they couldn't let anyone get away with less, unless it were to be a posting to some such paradise as Bermuda or peace-time Malta.

Nevertheless, despite not having met any of my new shipmates before, and probably because of the very close living association within the confines of the ship, I soon fitted in and felt at home.

There ensued much activity almost as soon as I was acclimatised, and the 'buzz' was that we were off to sea for some exercises with the rest of the Home Fleet. Sure enough, we (or at least the matelots of the appropriate division or department) removed the cables which tied us to the jetty, and I was off in my private yacht down the Tamar River.

The first task was to fly-on the aircraft, which were ashore, either at RAF Gosport or the seaplane station at Lee-on-Solent. There's something really thrilling about a ship the size of FURIOUS when it's steaming along at about thirty knots; the whole vessel vibrates as if alive - and I think it is - the wind blows dead in line with the course of the vessel to give the aircraft the minimum variation of their speed with that of the ship, and the ship is kept into wind by using a steam-jet right on the nose, sorry, the stem of the ship. The finest place to see and enjoy all this activity is, of course, in the nets which are erected alongside the flight deck for the safety of the attendant maintenance crews. These nets are formed of steel-wire cable with a mesh of about eight or nine inches, supported by a steel framework outboard and with a wooden plank about a foot wide attached to the bottom. When standing on the plank one's head is just above the level of the flightdeck, but it's on looking down that one really gets a thrill. Looked at from the front, a vessel like FURIOUS is wedge-shaped. From keel to flightdeck it is some eighty feet, and the deck must have been sixty feet wide, so that when looking directly down from the nets the waterline was some fifteen to twenty feet INBOARD from where you were, out above the water!

By the time that all the aircraft had flown on as we sailed up the Channel, we were off the Isle of Wight, and dropped the hook in the Solent. The whole ship's company was divided more or less equally into two parts, known as watches, Port and Starboard; it was very rare for both watches to be allowed shore leave at the same time; when the ship was in dry dock could be one case. On this occasion shore leave was piped up for the watch I belonged to and I put on my 'Best Blue' for my first trip ashore since joining the ship. A ladder was fixed from the port gunwale about midships and we proceeded down this to the boat awaiting our transport shore. This was a more or less open topped motor-driven boat with two canvas dodgers somewhat similar to the canvas hoods often used on RAF pick-up trucks, but of course larger. There were seats around this boat, but as what seemed to me like all the ship's crew came down the ladder, there was little chance of anyone actually sitting down. Packed like sardines, except we were standing up and not lying head to tail, there were over one hundred bods in that boat. The gunwales were nearly awash, or so it seemed to me, and the matelots thought nothing of it. However, even the hardy old salts were going to lose some sweat tonight. As we were approaching Gosport at the end of our nearly two mile trip, we met one of the new fast motor torpedo boats, which were produced near Southampton, out on sea tests with a civilian crew. It must have been deliberate, perhaps someone on board it had had a run-in with the Navy, but they opened up as they approached and the wash from that vessel damned near capsized us, or that was how it felt to the newly salted landlubber. One good thing came of it - my confidence in R.N. small boats was well reinforced, and I never bothered about how many bods got on board after that episode.

Apart from a little spray dampening on the way ashore, nothing of note springs to mind about that evening ashore; a few drinks in Pompey, perhaps a meal somewhere. It was quite often the case that we would stay ashore overnight at that haven for benighted sailors - Aggie Weston's - a good clean kip-down for no more than the cost of a couple of pints, and an early morning cuppa in time to catch the morning liberty boat. All the home ports had an Aggie Weston: Pompey, Guz and Chatham. Rosyth and Invergordon may have had one also, but I never heard them mentioned; and personally only sampled Guz (Devonport), and Pompey (Portsmouth). When in the Smoke (London), most lads used the Union Jack Club, which was open to all three Services. No doubt this still offers bed and breakfast to the troops, but not these days at one shilling and sixpence.

One interesting job which I was allocated during this first cruise was the construction of a crash trolley for use on the flight deck should an aircraft 'land' with sufficient gravitational force to render its undercarriage U/S. This trolley was to be a low aspect steel framework with four castor action wheels at the corners; the aircraft could than be lifted onto it - by hand - and the ensemble pushed on to the forward lift for rapid removal from the landing deck without the damage which would have been caused by just dragging it off the deck. After taking the aircraft down on the lift to the lower hangar, it could then be taken off the lift forward where there was an area large enough to accommodate a Swordfish. This area was in fact a storage area for our spare engines, two Pegasus and a Kestrel in cases, and was known as the aircraft repair shop but never used as such. The airlock passage which I mentioned earlier as becoming my own particular 'cabin' lay between this forward area and the E.R.S., and immediately aft of the double watertight doors was a large hatch which led directly down to the depths of the ship about three decks down, to the torpedo-fitters' workshop. I discovered this quite by accident, when one day my toolbox disappeared after I'd been doing a check on the spare engines. This toolbox was unique, and I just caught a glimpse of it when looking down the hatchway. It took me nearly an hour to find my way through the ship to that workshop to claim the box. The box was unique because screwed to its lid was a cast-brass facsimile of a Phoenix Head, which was the crest of HMS FURIOUS. Each of the blanking caps which covered the muzzles of our 5½ inch guns was embellished with this crest, and it was used in various other parts of the ship and its attendant small boats.

There was a large example of the crest fitted on top of the capstan which stood on the forward cable locker flat, which had been originally fitted to the 'bung' of the 18 inch gun with which Furious had been armed when first designed as a cruiser in 1915. When the forward 18 inch gun had been replaced by a landing-on deck in 1918, someone must have transferred the crest rather than scrap it. But it was not until 1925 that she was reconstructed as a flush-deck carrier, when she must have looked rather similar to her appearance in 1937.

At this juncture, I'd better give the reader some idea of the general geography and layout of this great steel town which was to be my home for some time to come. Firstly, by flush-deck, I meant that the flying-off/landing deck was free of superstructure, at least whilst flying was in progress. There were two bridges forward of the forward lift - one might say on either side of the front end of the deck - these bridges were flush with the deck when aircraft were flying, but could be raised hydraulically otherwise. The port bridge was usually the province of the RAF C/O and the starboard bridge was used to con the ship. A good word that, con, in this case it means to direct steering of the ship, to control all its movements and actions, and the officer who had this task certainly needed to study - or con - the ship. There were none of the funnels or smokestacks which most carriers and all other steamships have; instead the exhaust gases from the oil-fired boilers were vented through a large grating in the after end of the flight deck when aircraft were not flying on or off. There was an unusual arrangement whereby the gases were directed out from either side through alternative ducts; the consequence of this was that the after end of the ship became coated in soot. Not much to the liking of His Majesty's Royal Navy who like everything 'tiddley' - and why not! - so the whole of the back end was painted black so that the soot didn't show. During a refit in 1939 a small superstructure was erected which included a normal funnel and bridge etc., but this I never saw, and think that I should not have liked the old flat-top being made to look just like any other carrier. When she was recommissioned in May 1939, they had also taken out her ten 5½ inch guns and given her a dozen four inch high-angle anti-aircraft jobs. In view of the succeeding five years' adventures, this must have been a definite advantage; and certainly, of all the carriers which we had in 1939, she was the only one to see the War through, God bless her.

Going back to my mention of the ship's crest on the capstan, perhaps I should explain that the cable which was wound in by this capstan was a very large-linked chain for the forward anchor, and the 'flat' was the deck along which this 'cable' was laid out in rows when the anchor was inboard. This deck was on the same level as the E.R.S. workshop but sloped upwards slightly towards the bow.

Above it was another deck which started level with the upper hangar deck and sloped gently downward to join the cable deck at the bow.

This deck was known as the fore flying-off deck, because at some time before I had joined ship, aircraft had been able to fly off down this deck direct from the hangar. Common sense had obviously prevailed and in my time the hangar doors really were shut! That's a RAF term for not talking shop outside working hours. This pair of doors were angled together like canal lock gates, to obviate being bashed in by heavy seas I was told; seeing that the upper hangar deck must have been about thirty feet above water level I took that tale with a grain of salt, but before being much older I was to see water coming over the bow and belting up that deck!

Mounted on the fore flying deck were a pair of anti-aircraft 3.7 in guns, and also a pair of multiple pom-poms. These were 2 pounder machine guns with ammunition in continuous belts like a 303 Browning or Vickers, and mounted in two pairs one above the other, to be fired as one gun. These interesting weapons were known to irreverent erks as 'Chicago pianos'.

One of the objects of this autumn cruise, apart from a flying programme, was to be a Home Fleet gunnery practice, and I found this quite exciting. There were all the usual sort of routine jobs to do, and these kept us in the workshop for much of the time. There were morning break periods of ten or so minutes for a smoke outside the workshop. This area was part of a six feet or so gangway running most of the length of the ship, and at intervals along it were installed the main armament of 5½ inches, one of which was immediately outside our E.R.S., where a sponson - a sort of bay window construction - gave more space for the gun; this area was where we could smoke during official break periods and when off duty.

CHAPTER 7
An Autumn Cruise

We were somewhere in the North Sea one day and, although I was aware that some other ships were in the vicinity, I was busy at my bench working on the crash trolley I mentioned earlier. I suddenly noticed that I was alone in the workshop, but was at an interesting point in the job and just thought, "It must be break time or something, I'll just finish this bit." I very soon learned where and why they had disappeared - there was an almighty crash just outside about six feet from my bench and I thought the End of the World had come. But it wasn't, it was just that gun. All my seasoned shipmates had known what to expect and forgot to tell me. Needless to say, it was not long before I dropped tools and rapidly made my way as far from the gun as possible. Actually, I made my way to the flight deck where I found most of my HQ Flight comrades enjoying the sight of the Home Fleet in line astern. Immediately astern was Warspite, a battleship with fifteen in guns, and everywhere we looked there was something new to see.

At about five miles away to port there was a largish ship steaming on a parallel course to ours. This, I was told, was HMS Centurion, an oldish cruiser which was used as a target ship, a rather expensive form of target I thought, but I was reassured by my shipmates; it had been rendered more or less immune to puncture by judicious use of reinforced concrete and was practically unsinkable. As she had a volunteer crew aboard to service the engine-room, etc., that was just as well with large lumps of ordnance flying in its general direction. I say general direction because the idea was not to actually HIT the target but to aim so many degrees off - shoot, as the system was so lucidly described.

It must be admitted that the lads did warn me of what was due to happen at any minute now, but I was completely unprepared for the effect that the firing of all five port guns in a broadside discharge had on the ship and my ears. Although we were on the flight deck, the instantaneous firing of five guns seemed even more than just five times the effect of that first one when I had been only feet away from the breech. And not only the sound, the ship heeled over to starboard at about fifteen degrees which really surprised me. A good side wind made her heel over a bit, not surprising considering the great length and height of her slab-sided conformation, but for five smallish bags of burning cordite grains to be able to push out lumps of steel called shells for several miles AND to shove that great ship over by reactive force at the same time was awe-inspiring.

When it came to the turn of the battlewaggon, Warspite I think, but it may have been Ramilles, to fire her fifteen-inch jobs, they made our little effort seem like sparklers at a firework display. Centurion had moved away and then we guessed her to be all of ten miles away. Warspite raised those two pairs of turretted guns to around fifteen to twenty degrees and fired them separately towards Centurion over to port. The first visual impact was a great gout of flame, orange to red and about fifty yards long, which rapidly ended in a solid cloud of whitish smoke which would have covered a football pitch. The passage of the ship soon dispersed and left behind the smoke cloud, but the noise wasn't left behind, a good lightning strike ten feet away may be compared with it. But the amazing part of this to me was that we could actually SEE the shell on its trajectory, and it was glowing faintly red from the heat generated by its passage through the air and partly, perhaps, transferred from that damn great flame; there was also what appeared to be a whitish smoke trail, which may have been vorticular condensation caused by its passage. The passage of our own shot had been missed because the heeling over had hidden it from our view, but when we later did a night shoot, then that too glowed with its passage and looked even brighter at night.

This 'shoot' or gunnery practice was being undertaken by the whole Home Fleet and naturally took quite some days. I don't recall exactly how long, but it was certainly in no way monotonous. When the main armament had had their full quota of exercise, it was the turn of the lighter weapons designed to be used against aircraft. Had the Navy been more clairvoyant these weapons would have had priority, for there was to come a time not far ahead when even the big guns would be used against aircraft. However, aeroplanes were still regarded by the Andrew as just one more bloody nuisance, and looked at from their angle perhaps it was justifiable. They _were_ in the process of being converted, many of the aircrew even in 1937 were matelots, Officer pilots and Telegraphist/Air gunner ranks, but when I was relieved in January 1939, it was by the first Naval aircraft artificer to join FURIOUS.

To return to the shoot; the port and starboard 4.7 Ack Ack or High Angle/Low Angle guns as the Navy called them, had had a few rounds off in the general direction of the target aircraft without much excitement, as had most of the rest of the Fleet one supposes. The reader has to realise that the day to day work of the section was continuing fairly normally during working hours and often outside them.

When multiple pom-poms were given the opportunity to fill the sky with their 2 lb shells they really excelled themselves and brought proceedings to an unexpected halt. The target in this case was a de Haviland Gypsy Moth, a light biplane, often used by the RAF as an *ab initio* trainer; except that in this case it was radio controlled from one of the county class cruisers, probably HMS Norfolk. A group of us from HQ Flight were on deck during this little effort and the 'Queen Bee', as it was called, flew along to port for the Chicago piano to give them a tune. They did; instead of aiming off as was the drill, they either had the devil in them and thought now's the chance to get at those crabfat matelots, or they were just inexperienced and rotten shots. The net result was one Queen Bee with no further flying career, damaged beyond repair - and in the drink to boot!

Soon after the Fleet exercise we were sailing northwards up the North Sea with quite a blow on, the ship was rolling slightly and pitching a bit more than slightly, with waves coming over the bows fairly often. Just aft of that crested capstan aforementioned was a little cubbyhole wherein dwelt eventimes when we were at sea, a three-badge matelot who sold soft drinks by the glass to those who were strolling up and down the cable locker flat just for exercise or a change of scenery and a smoke. This innocuous beverage he called a gopher, just why that name I never found out. Nowadays, I believe that real beer is available to the lower deck personnel, but they don't have the advantage of a free issue of rum. Rum for Chief and Petty Officers that is, the daily ration which was issued to we lesser mortals was watered down to some extent and known as grog, after an admiral of the distant past who had initiated the watering-down process of the free issue. Even then the issue was much to be preferred to the alternative threepence per day in lieu, as it was a fifth of a pint of fifty-fifty water. Senior NCO's were allowed to receive their ration neat, and although many of them tended to save a few days' issue and have a little binge, that was not officially approved of.

On this stormy night I ventured forward of the gopher bar just for the thrill of feeling the ship's movement; the deep throb of the engines could be felt through the deck plates and there were great shudders up there at the sharp end when the heavy seas bashed against the stem, to send heavy spray along the cable flat deck. This was not a recommended practice, an extra large wave could wash a man overboard or knock him down, but all I got was a soaking.

I was to get another soaking on this cruise - perhaps less deservedly.

We, the ship that is, sailed into the Moray Firth and passed though the Sutors of Cromarty, to anchor in the Cromarty Firth off Invergordon for a few days. One day a football match was organised between two of the Flights, and every bod who was not on watch was expected to give the hardy players some support. So we did, we took rattles and a gas alarm hand-bell, greatcoats - it was November - plenty of enthusiasm and a damn good thirst.

One fellow who was not too happy later was our Flight-Sergeant. A goal was scored by one side or other, it didn't really matter which, and a lad named Tex Rickard, who had the hand-bell, became a bit overexcited and, instead of just ringing it, he emulated all those who were flinging their caps in the air; that would have been of little note if Chiefy's head had not been in the way when it fell to earth. There was no permanent damage but he did have a headache for the rest of the day. This Tex was a member of a rugby team in our home port of Devonport, and some time after our return to Guz he had his jaw broken in a match, not by Chiefy I hasten to add; his lower jaw was wired up nicely and we had to feed him on Scotch broth for a few days.

Whilst we were at anchor in the Cromarty Firth, our Wing Commander took it into his head to throw a party for as many of his command as could be spared from duty and who so wished. To this end he organised a meal at an hotel in Dingwall, and most of us who were able sailed off down the Firth in liberty boats.

During the course of the meal, the Winco gave a little speech which included a joke in the usual tradition. Without being too long-winded, this joke was about a music-hall act where a man was giving a demonstration of his act to his agent and in the process he fell off the stage into the orchestra stalls. Picking himself up and staggering onto the stage holding his head on one side he asked, in a constricted tone of voice, "How was that then, will it do?"

"That'll do fine," was the reply, "but you can cut out the pansy stuff!"

"Pansy stuff be damned, I've broken my bloody neck!" croaked the performer.

To the reader, this may not seem a very funny story, but coming from Noakes, our Winco, it was hilarious, for he too had suffered a broken neck. When a fighter pilot during the '14-18 War, he had crashed, or been shot down, in France and sustained a broken neck which caused him to hold his head on one side and restricted his speech a little.

Later, when the RAF component of the ship's company was ashore at RAF Donibristle in Fifeshire, we were to see a demonstration of his flying skill, broken neck or not. It was some time in the summer, July or August of 1938, and one of the new Hurricane fighters visited us, probably for refuelling. The Winco naturally had to try this aircraft; it must have been a great temptation after our Ospreys, or even the Nimrods which had preceded them. I suppose the visiting pilot couldn't bring himself to refuse Jackie and so he was able to show us just what he and a Hurrybird could do. During one of his passes across the 'drome, he must have noticed that one of the hangars had both doors wide open - and this was the only time that I ever saw an aeroplane fly straight through an aircraft hangar. He got a good cheer from us erks even if the C/O of Doni may not have approved!

There was a general buzz (rumour) current among the RAF lads that our C/O wouldn't mind breaking his neck again, so that it could be reset straight, but maybe that could be classed as libel!

The second soaking for me of the cruise occurred after the Dingwall party when trying to board the liberty-boat from a slime-encrusted jetty, whilst the boat was going up and down about six feet with the tidal wash. As the crew could not actually tie up to the jetty like rowing boats on the Serpentine, we had to time things right and jump when the boat was nearest to us. Being just a crabfat matelot and with more than enough ale aboard, when I jumped the boat had moved somewhere else and I landed in the 'oggin. Not to worry overmuch, the boat's crew were real sailors and they hooked me out almost before I got my shirt wet, and definitely before I was flattened between the boat and jetty. But I did swallow a modicum of salt water and the first thing I did after climbing up the ladder on board FURIOUS was to have my first and only bout of sea-sickness.

CHAPTER 8
Ashore

Coming south again from Scotland, the aircraft were flown off to Gosport and we steamed on to Guz and a spot of Christmas leave. Not actual leave in this case; in pre-war RAF there were often what were known as 'grants' at Christmas, Easter, Whitsuntide and even the August bank holiday weekend - not every national Bank Holiday and never more than five days (but with judicious use of weekend passes this could be stretched to nine with a kind orderly room chief!), and only at the C/O's discretion if those 'exigencies of the Services' allowed.

Annual leave of 28 days was usual in the RAF; this was not encroached upon by grants and most Units permitted it to be taken at request, in weeks or all at once, subject of course to those exigencies! The Navy, and thus the Fleet Air Arm had six weeks annual, so that we 'guests' also copped for six weeks - plus any grants going when at Guz or ashore - the best of both worlds indeed.

The food on board, at sea or against the wall, was far better than normal RAF rations, though the system was a bit tiresome to people used to just walking into the cookhouse and collecting food from a hatch.

Our HQ Flight mess-deck above the E.R.S. contained three tables athwartships, suspended from the deckhead at one end and hinged to the starboard bulkhead at the other. Above the bulkhead end was a shelved locker in which mess members kept personal items such as butter (never margarine), marmalade, tinned fruit, etc.

At the 'free' end was a large (polished, of course!) metal box which contained communal rations, viz. tea, tinned milk, sugar and blocks of raw cocoa with lumps of cocoa butter admixed. To make 'Kai', our last drink before retiring, one scraped a sufficient quantity from the block, added a tin of Nestle's condensed milk and then duty cook toddled off with the dixie to the galley to fill it up with hot water. Great stuff, especially with a tot of rum in it on a winter's evening.

There were wooden plank-covered gangways either side of the ship which stretched from just forward of our E.R.S. right aft to the quarterdeck, and the galley or cookhouse in Air Force parlance, was seventy or so feet aft along the port side. Immediately opposite the galley door was the gash-shoot, which was a contrivance which looked like a ship's ventilator in reverse, attached to the bulwark. It was about two feet square opening inboard with a canvas tube like a modern-day airliner's emergency exit hanging over the side to just above the waterline. One could perhaps describe this construction as the refuse-disposal department for the ship's company. To keep it reasonably clean and free from blockages, the inside was fitted with plumbing similar to that found in public toilets. Of course when against the wall or in dry dock there were other means of disposal for 'gash'.

Whether or not that Christmas leave was part of my annual or a grant, I'm afraid eludes me. I expect that it was enjoyed, as leave mostly was, even when life in the old home town was not as exciting as everyday work in the RAF. There was one episode during this leave when Hard-Done-By and myself managed to get ourselves evicted from the stalls bar of the local Hippodrome, and all we'd done was spray ourselves and the barmaid with soda syphons. This was more hilarious than acrimonious, but slightly disgraceful nonetheless.

Back at the ship in Guz Harbour, it was soon apparent that movement was afoot. The rumour going round was that we were off to the Mediterranean for a spring and summer cruise; somebody perhaps had seen a load of light-grey paint come aboard! What was certain was that a large amount of RAF stores were turning up and needing homes. To this end, we moved back against the wall so that the dockyard cranes could be utilised, instead of lighters bringing gear out to us, and having to use the cranes either side of the quarterdeck just aft of the after hangar doors.

There were some aspects of the character of Plymouth dockies which could give one the idea that they were geniuses, and other aspects that gave one the impression that they should be locked away in 'Colney Hatch'. One day a consignment of spare mainplanes arrived for Swordfish in this case and HQ Flight had some bods on the quay and some on the quarterpatch to fit the slings by which a dockyard crane would lift them aboard. I was in the shore party and when slings were fitted to the first mainplane the crane, which was one of those tall derrick types, whistled it up to swing round and lower it to our quarterdeck. Snag was, there was a fair old breeze blowing off-shore and the dockie on the crane took his load up so far that the wind caught it, and the cable plus mainplane went out at an angle of about forty-five degrees from the vertical; perhaps no one had told him that aircraft wings were meant to fly. It took the inboard team some hair-raising effort to get that mainplane aboard without wrecking it, and further lifts were postponed until the wind dropped a few points.

This taking on of stores was quite a busy time. In the days before FURIOUS had been converted to oil burning, coaling ship had been undertaken by all personnel, and that included Naval officers I was told. I must say that I didn't see many of them hauling sides of beef up the gangways on this occasion. One item - or rather a group of items - which came aboard was a complete workshop toolkit for the Rolls Kestrels of our Ospreys, but more of that later.

Towards the end of January, we moved out to tie on to a buoy in the Tamar Estuary and the ship's company began to shake down and prepare for sea. This is not quite like putting out in a forty-foot yacht, where one just unties a bit of rope, starts up any engine one may have and casts off. With a large naval vessel, it entails the change-over from shore-based services such as electrical power, bread baking, even sewage disposal, to our own self-contained inboard organisational systems. While this process was taking place, communication with the shore was undertaken by our faithful servant, the drifter 'Noontide'. From the build of her and of course the designation - drifter - her designed job in life was casting out netting and pulling in enough herring to pay her way, but I don't think she had been engaged so for a long time.

When at sea we were accompanied by a more warlike vessel, a much faster one, HMS Keith, a destroyer. Keith kept station, usually to starboard and about a couple of cables aft, especially when aircraft were operating, but she was never far away. On the autumn cruise with the Home Fleet during the very heavy weather we'd experienced (at least I'd thought it heavy!), I remember looking over to starboard and seeing Keith's running lights appear and disappear with sickening irregularity and equally sickening changes of attitude. The only comment to make was, "God help the sailors on a night like this."

There was, I recall, just one liberty for each watch, before we got underway and trickled gently into Plymouth Sound, and moved into the Channel. The 'buzz' was that before taking on the aircraft, we were going to indulge in a little fun - speed trials no less.

This exercise was proceeding apace (no pun intended), with the old flat-top careering along at thirty-three knots, when we slowed down to a rather more sedate pace. The explanation we were given over the tannoy was that a fault had arisen in the steering engine. There was one excellent aspect of life aboard one of His Majesty's ships, and that was that we were always, or nearly always, told what was going on, and when we were not then someone who knew would usually spread the word. On this occasion the information was fairly accurate; we had apparently suffered a rather serious crack in the bed-plate of the steering engine, and the result was that speed trials were suspended and we were back to Guz at a very gentle pace for a check-up.

Having returned to Plymouth and dropped the hook in the Sound, it was not long before we were again land-locked. This time the ship was put into the dry dock at Devonport, a very interesting procedure; life is never tedious with the Royal Navy!

It took some time of course, there was very little spare room within the dock as we were eased into it, and then the great gates were closed and our seven hundred or so feet were trapped. And now the dockies really came into their own; the ship was shored up with great baulks of timber so that she remained in the upright position, and when that was accomplished to the complete satisfaction of the chief bowler-hatted gentleman, then the water was pumped out of the dock and left us high - comparatively - and dry within our new prison.

Now was the time that knowledgeable and opportunist matelots came into their own. As the water receded in the dock giving more room for more timber stays, so thick mud on the bottom became visible and in that mud considerable livestock was being stranded. One item I watched a couple of seamen 'collect' was a conger eel about ten feet long, which must have been nine or ten inches in diameter and a mouth filled with teeth like a barbed wire fence which could have bitten a man's arm off - given the chance, which it wasn't. Conger eel is quite a delicacy and some seamen must have dined well that day and some subsequent ones.

With the three operational Flights ashore with their aircraft at Gosport, the only RAF still aboard were we forty-eight members of

HQ Flight, and for us life was not quite as good as previously. Being in dry dock meant, among other snags, that the ship's boilers were closed down except for some sort of auxiliary heating and the big electric generators were also at rest. We couldn't use the ship's heads (toilet facilities) and needed to go ashore for calls of nature.

This need did occasion one weirdly funny episode, which bears the telling. The toilets on the dockside were arranged in a long row of ten to fifteen cubicles, with plain wooden seats and one long channel connecting all, with a common flushing cistern at one end. One day some practical joker lit a sheet of paper at the cistern end just prior to a flush, and disappeared rapidly before the howls of anguish and rage from occupied cubicles heralded dire consequences for the culprit.

We were soon invaded by what were known as dockyard labourers or dockies for short, but who were more often highly skilled artisans who were capable of taking a ship apart and putting it back together in the time it would take some present-day workers to think about it. However libellous that may be, it was not long before a large hole appeared in the upper hanger deck with a corresponding one in the lower hanger deck. Investigation by curious erks disclosed that the holes were continuing down through the ship as if they were building another lift-well beside the existing after one. It must be said that some satisfaction was gained by noting that this great hole passed right through the part of the ship which was occupied by officers. One of the few bones of contention between officers and other ranks in any of our three Services was always the inordinate amount of space and facilities which the former occupied vis-à-vis non-commissioned ranks. The area of this great ship which the forty-eight members of HQ Flight were officially allocated would just about garage two medium sized motor-cars - or four cavalry-sized horses, if the trucks used to transport troops during the '14-18 War (forty men or eight horses) are comparable.

It could perhaps be argued that this discrepancy of treatment was just the privilege of rank, but it could be equally pleaded that privilege should be earned. Whichever way one looks at it the system has, over many years, proved to breed a type of serviceman who are more than the equal of any other nation, whether sleeping in feather-bedded bunks or hammocks.

One item of our lives which was not adversely affected by the sojourn in dry dock was the food; this continued to be pretty good.

Perhaps a little dissertation wouldn't come amiss here. As already said, the mess deck was furnished with three tables, guaranteed not to shift when at sea, and on either side of each were forms, for airmen to sit down on. Underneath, incidentally was a shelf which was, I was told, intended for the storage of spare pairs of shoes. Digressing once more, because the Navy were allowed shoes for shore leave, so were we 'guests' - this had something to do with warm weather wear, ships not being confined to latitudes above 50° North.

From time to time as required - literally - the mess deck was issued with a bag of potatoes, which were kept in one corner as much out of the way as was possible. Every evening after supper, members of the mess were expected to peel just as many spuds as they considered would fit their appetite on the following day, and were honour-bound to take just that amount and no more. It was a system which worked very well, there was no great task in peeling the spuds for one man, and the alternative would have been the sort of punishment fatigue which obtained in land-based Services. Each of the three tables constituted a separate group, and each day elected - on a roster, of course - a duty cook. The duty cook didn't do much in the cooking line but it was his duty to collect the cooked food for each meal from the galley, and to dish it out to the lads in the mess deck. He also probably had the task of washing the plates and utensils but this is where my memory fails me - I can't ever remember washing eating irons or plates, but must have done so often. There was a canteen, run by the NAAFI via a civilian employee who lived aboard. I've wondered since, what happened during wartime; the Navy probably enlisted him in the manner of Nelson's press gangs. From this canteen, all manner of food could be purchased; there was always a queue there during opening hours, mostly for chocolate bars and cigarettes. Tobacco products, of course, were duty-free, and unlike modern day duty-free shops in ferries and airports, they really were free of duty. As an example, Players' Navy Cut were twenty for sixpence. Many of the crew made their own cigarettes from tobacco which could be purchased monthly in either leaf form or cut ready for rolling, at a ration of half a pound per month for one shilling and sixpence. Weird, but not wonderful, were the stories of what long-serving matelots did with issue leaf and their rum issues to fit it for pipe smoking.

One good aspect of being in dry dock, or against the wall for that matter, was that laundry facilities ashore were available. This was normal practice in the RAF ashore; a contractor called at the station once a week, brought one's clean dhobi back reasonably pressed and collected a soiled set. The same procedure happened when ships were in port. But at sea, one did one's own dhobi; there was a steam-filled area in the bowels of the ship where one could have a shower and wash clothes at the same time. One snag attached to this was that the water was SALT, and ordinary soap just refused to raise a lather with the stuff that fishes swim in; we had to use a special seawater soap, and hard graft it made washing one's clothes.

It was very soon apparent that with little or no work to do, at least for we fitters and Jack Oyler, the coppersmith, etc., the Navy would want us out of their way or the RAF would find work for us. And so it turned out.

We did manage to stay aboard long enough to trip over spanners welded to decks by practical-joking dockies and to take part in gin rummy games with some of them in odd corners of the ship, and also to see the great steel casting of the cracked steering-engine bed-plate being hauled out from the bottom of the ship; that load didn't swing in the wind!

The order came through, and we were all parcelled off to Gosport with the rest of the RAF component of the ship's company.

We were not really sorry to leave Devonport dockyard and the old flat-top. With the ship lying dead and fairly cold in dry dock, with our home invaded by civvies, most of the crew were spending much time ashore. Aggie Weston's was a popular place for spending the night rather than wandering back through the dockyard, tripping over railway lines and walking into gantry cranes and suchlike. It was with little regret then that HQ Flight heard that we were to join the rest at Gosport.

As soon as we had settled in, one of the first jobs I was detailed for was to change the engine of one of the Swordfish.

This kind of work was the main task of an engine repair shop on most RAF stations; and an aircraft-carrier was equivalent to a land-based unit with several squadrons operating therefrom. One-hundred-and-twenty hour inspections and engine changes were not the best use of ground staff when a unit had a full flying programme to fulfil.

Changing an engine was a pleasant and enjoyable task, and doing the job as a solo task gave one a real boost to the morale. Of course, it was always expected that advice should be sought when necessary, and the maintenance manuals could be consulted when any snag cropped up.

Time was really no taskmaster just so long as one did the work with reasonable dispatch, and that when finished it stood up to the requirement of absolute reliability; that was ALL that was necessary! So, after three weeks or so, that Swordfish was complete with a nice new Pegasus engine with everything locked neatly, oil tank filled with DTD 109, fuel tank full and, after a little hesitation (on the engine's part), and a cloud of blue smoke from the burning off of what remained in the cylinders of corrosion inhibitor, it was given a good ground testing. It only remained to sign the relevant parts of the 700 (record of an aircraft's maintenance and inspections), get our sergeant fitter to check everything and also sign-up; then we needed a pilot to air-test it.

This being arranged, I stood by the kite - with 700 ready for the pilot's inspection - ready to start up when he arrived on the tarmac.

When the pilot appeared, he was a Naval Lieutenant, carrying the usual type of parachute, the 'chute pack attached to the harness and designed to be used as a seat padding. The driving seats of service aeroplanes were just metal basin-shapes designed to accept this type of 'chute, and were damned uncomfortable for ground crews to sit on without a parachute.

As he came up to the aircraft and examined the 700, he said, "I see she's had a new engine fitted, who did the job?"

With not a little pride, I replied, "I did, Sir."

"Well go and get yourself a parachute then, it'll be lonely up there."

I waited not upon the order of my going, but scampered off to the parachute store like a dog with two tails, etc. When I returned, I placed the 'chute pack in the rear cockpit, where it was secured to the side with a pair of elastic ropes, putting on the harness over my overalls. This harness was fitted with a pair of quick-fastening hooks at the front designed to accept a matching pair of steel rings which were fitted to the 'chute pack: the theory was that it would take but a moment to attach the pack to the harness in an emergency. Also, as a means of staying aboard the kite when it strayed from an even keel etc., there was a third ring in the backside area, the purpose of which was to receive a clip on the upper end of a steel cable about 30 cwt breaking strain, the lower end of which was attached firmly to the deck of the rear cockpit. Two people could stand in that rear cockpit of the Swordfish, so there was plenty of room for one bod to move around in it, and plenty of slack in the cable to allow such movement.

The 700 being signed up, back in the flight office, I fixed the starting handle in position and called out, "Switches off, fuel on," then proceeded to wind up the inertia-starter. This was a heavy flywheel gadget which stored up energy as it revolved faster and faster under the influence of bods turning the handle. One could tell when sufficient energy was available from experience, by the sound it made as it built up speed; at that pitch, the ground crew called out, "Contact", and pulled on a cable passing through the cowling to engage the starter flywheel with the engine crankshaft, at the same time winding vigorously on the hand-starter magneto. With luck, the engine fired, and one could then dry the sweat generated by the winding, in the slipstream developed by the airscrew. A hand-starter mag. wasn't always necessary when an engine was warm, but ensured that a good spark was available just when most needed and the engines' two magnetos were revolving too slowly to provide one. Most aircraft were also equipped with a Ki-gas pump which could supply a small quantity of petrol to each cylinder - it was a long way from the carburettor to the top cylinders!

Enough of that; when the Peggy was running nicely, I clambered in to the rear cockpit and clipped the 'dog-chain' to the ring of my parachute harness. The wheel chocks I'd already removed, and we taxied out for the take off. After a gentle climb over Gosport to about five thousand and with the engine still not fallen off, the driver stuck his hand above his head and twisted it about whilst he grinned at me over his shoulder - naturally I grinned back - I was really enjoying life; there had been few opportunities for flips at Thornaby for we always seemed too busy keeping the kites flying for luckier folk.

Having obtained my affirmative, we went into a most interesting and exciting regime; I knew the Swordfish was a toughie, and an ordinary loop would not overstrain it or the crew, but a slow roll was quite a strain on my nerves. The retaining dog-chain had about six inches of leeway to allow the Telegraphist/Air-gunner to move around in the performance of his duties, but of course, attacking enemy ships with a torpedo or defending the aircraft with the Lewis gun didn't usually entail inverted flying. To cap my terror, we remained inverted for rather longer than during a normal slow roll and I was gripping the sides of the cockpit very tightly - just in case that thin cable broke or came unstuck. I needn't have worried, it would have supported six of me.

After what must have been an hour at least, but seemed only minutes to me, of flying over the Isle of Wight, we were at about four and a half thousand above the Solent when my pilot spotted a big freighter sailing up the Solent towards Southampton. He turned round to me and pointed over the side at this ship with a questioning expression on his face, as much as to say, "Do you see that fellow?" I nodded back and was rather surprised by the result. We went into about a thirty degree dive and within a very short time were flying alongside that freighter - and looking UP at its cheering crew. It wouldn't surprise me to learn that that Lieutenant was among the crews who attacked the Italians in Taranto Harbour some years later.

Some time in March or April of 1938, while the whole RAF complement was at Gosport, the ship was recommissioned - at least the RAF part of it did; the poor old ship herself was still in dock at Guz having its steering engine put back into operation - and probably sundry other work while it was lying helpless. There were a lot of postings into Gosport and a lot of postings away, but not one for me; I was left to finish my full time in the FAA, and was quite pleased about it too. Incidentally, this was when I discovered that once a Fleet Air Arm man, it was often repeated; several of the new men were not only ex-FAA but a number had actually served in FURIOUS. This bore out the feeling that was growing in my mind by now that this Airforce was a kind of selective club of which I was quite 'chuffed' to be a member.

Not much after the change-over of personnel, we were moved as a body to Scotland; a complete train was engaged and the whole four flights were embarked. I've only ridden on one worse train journey than that one, and that was in a French train in 1939, of which more perhaps later. This particular train was apparently in no great hurry to get anywhere, let alone Scotland. We were in it for over twenty-four hours, and just about the worst part of the journey was being in a siding within sight of York Station and just left there - on that curve at York which has the rails banked like Brooklands - for literally hours.

It was almost impossible to sit still, because one kept sliding along the seat!

All things end eventually, and the train passed over the Forth Bridge to dump us in the wilds of the Kingdom of Fife, where we disembarked for our new temporary home, RAF Donibristle.

Nostalgic visiting is not really a very satisfactory occupation; I passed where the entrance gates used to be some years ago and Doni, like Thornaby, is now a housing estate.

CHAPTER 9
Donibristle

There were advantages and otherwise attached to being shore-based; we most certainly had more room for living and working in, and having some distance between billet and workshop a deal more exercise. That last proved to be one of the disadvantages - there was a policy among the indigenous hierarchy to ensure that everyone was kept fit - and they instituted early morning PT for all. The usual programme was a brisk run around the perimeter of the aerodrome which seemed to last until the PT instructor himself was tired. An excellent prelude to the run was the availability of a bucket of tea for each hut who could muster a volunteer to fetch it. This was known by the odd name of 'Gunfire', and Doni B was not the only station where this good idea prevailed; perhaps it was a hang-up from '14-18 trench warfare, when the troops had to 'stand-to' at dawn in order to be shot at by gunfire and a mug of tea helped to make them feel bullet-proof!

Some interesting tasks were undertaken whilst at Doni B, and for at least two of them I was teamed up with one of the newly arrived fitters. Jim Greenwood had similar tastes in off-duty activity to myself, which, considering that his people kept a pub called the General Rawden in the oddly named town of Luddendenfoot, was not surprising.

One of the experiments with a fairly long programme was testing engine oil which we had run through a filter machine which was supposed to bring back used oil to its pristine condition. It was usual for the DTD 109 lubricating oil used in aircraft engines to be changed after forty hours' flying time, when it was beginning to show signs of discoloration. After being passed through this filtration plant the oil certainly looked like new and felt like new oil to the touch. The test programme envisaged was to use this oil for one of the Swordfish after an engine change and to compare the result against another Pegasus using new oil. By dismantling both engines after similar flying times, the amount of wear occurring in each would give an assessment. It was a few months later that Jim and I had the opportunity to compare the two affected engines, and we found that the filtered oil allowed far more wear to take place than new oil. Much later, post-War knowledge tells us that there is more to oil than carbon discoloration; the molecular construction changes its configuration, and breaks down earlier under load. Nowadays, of course, the oil industry has improved its product vastly with various additives, and we might not get the same result if we did the experiment again today.

In Inverkeithing Bay, just under the north end of the Forth Bridge the RAF had a high-speed launch station. They were used for jobs like target-towing, for the rescue of aircrew who ditched their craft and for acting as tenders to flying boats and seaplanes as necessary; lovely boats they were, with three Napier Lion aircraft engines for power. These Lions were almost identical to those used in aircraft like the Vickers Virginia; the main modification was a cast-iron crankcase in lieu of the usual aluminium one. Jim and I had the nice little job of giving one of these engines a top-overhaul, which passed time very pleasantly.

During one of our off-duty exploratory walks, Jim and I discovered a track of about two miles running alongside an old railway line. This track led us eventually to a small harbour affair with a dilapidated looking jetty, and on this jetty was a lonely little pub, which backed onto the Forth. It came to light during subsequent visits, that the jetty and line had been built in order that Royal Navy ships could conveniently be coaled direct from the mine, which was situated a few miles inland. Now that the great majority of vessels were oil-fired, it had fallen into disuse as a jetty and the pub itself was not greatly patronised. However, it had reasonable beer to sell, was at a distance which made the walk thirsty work, and to cap all, the landlady owner had three nubile daughters, and a large kitchen where there was often supper to add to the other attractions.

One Sunday afternoon, we met two middle-aged gentlemen, and became engaged in conversation with them - couldn't really help it actually, the pub was so small. These two often appeared there on other occasions, and nearly always insisted on buying the beer - why should we continue to refuse we thought, they obviously have money to spare, and at four-and-sixpence a day, our pay could well do with supplementing. This generosity continued for some weeks on and off; we were even treated to a weekend in Edinburgh, which included a tour of the excellent Art Gallery and, naturally, the Castle. However, it all came to a sticky end one night, when we were having a lift back to Camp in the car which they usually travelled to the pub in. As we pulled up outside the guard-room, I heard Jim curse in the back seat, there was a scuffle and he jumped out rapidly. He told me that his companion in the back had tried to open his trouser flies, and he'd reacted by thumping him - not a very friendly thing to do to someone who had always treated us both well. That put an end to our free beer, but not to the suppers in the kitchen of the Fordell Arms. It has occurred to me since that there must be something in the air around Edinburgh, or perhaps the wearing of kilts does more than just make the knees cold!

In pre-War days, May 24th was celebrated as Empire Day, certainly in Britain and very probably throughout the Colonies and Dominions. Such a celebration has now been rendered irrelevant and inappropriate as we have no Empire because of the actions of successive governments. The Commonwealth is not really a germane alternative body, especially in view of our now close involvement with European countries; which has increasingly damaged our erstwhile relationship with the Dominions, and driven them to make other alliances and trade agreements. However that may be, when we did have an Empire which we cared for, the RAF did its bit in remembering it. On the Saturday which fell nearest to May 24th, many of those peace-time stations in the British Islands were opened to the public for what was known as Empire Air Day, thus promoting general awareness of the Empire and indirectly assisting the finances of the RAF Benevolent Fund.

Doni B was not that year being opened for EAD - perhaps because it was in effect being rented out to the Navy - but the aerodrome near Edinburgh used by an Auxiliary Air Force unit, 603 Squadron, at Turnhouse was to be open.

It so happened that Doni B was but recently the lucky recipient of a brand new type of fire-tender, and it was decided to lend it to Turnhouse and show it off in public. This tender was totally different from the usual red-painted vehicle - it was battleship grey (appropriate at Donibristle with we grey-blue matelots in residence), and streamlined in design, something similar to the post-war Jowett Javelin motor car. It carried its own self-contained foam tank, and CO^2 gas cylinders for electric fires. The foam could be pumped to a pair of hoses which were stored either side of the driver's seat, folded neatly in steel boxes with padded lids for the crew's accommodation, in such a manner that each firecrew member could open his door, lift the lid and run out with the nozzle, and the hose would unfold nicely and freely behind him. The driver's part in this operation was to keep the engine running, to engage the foam pump and open the valves to the hose or hoses. The gearbox controls may have been slightly more complicated than those of a normal truck, but not beyond the capabilities of a RAF type. The CO^2 cylinders had their own hose of rather smaller bore in heavy black rubber material.

Donibristle had a permanent fire-crew under the command of a specialist corporal driver, but fire-pickets were still an occasional duty. On all stations one could find oneself liable to fire-picket, although only stations like Uxbridge had guard duties to contend with in peace-time.

Just how it was that I had the luck (or otherwise!) to be down for a fire-picket duty on that May day I don't recall; perhaps, with my fairly strong passion for the presence of aircraft, I found out what the possibilities were and actually volunteered. As it turned out, two of us picket crew were detailed to accompany the corporal driver in the new tender to Turnhouse. Who wouldn't be pleased about a nice long ride in a new vehicle, to an RAF station where one could expect to see an interesting flying programme, and also perhaps meet with sundry young Scots lassies!

The trip westward nearly to Stirling before we could cross the Forth, and back to Turnhouse was uneventful, apart from a stop for a pint en route, and on arrival at the 'drome we were detailed to park adjacent to the tarmac so that we could be seen by the public. The station, of course, had their own fire tender and ambulance more accessible to the flying area. As the day progressed we three crew took it in turns to wander around, and part of the wandering took us to the NAAFI canteen for the odd pint or cuppa; our driver friend was pretty well-known for his thirst - which may have had some bearing on his still being only a corporal despite a row of campaign medals of the Great War, and about twenty years' service.

All would have been well, and we should have departed with grateful thanks for our participation, but Fate intervened. The Air Officer commanding the group which Turnhouse came under, noticed this strange vehicle sitting on the tarmac, and in the nature of such gentlemen wished to learn more. The C.O. of the station equally naturally, decided to oblige him with a demonstration. He got it! Bear in mind that this vehicle had not been used in earnest, if at all, and although its part-time crew knew the theory of its operation, and might even have been useful in the event of a real fire occurring, we were a little in awe of being auditioned by all those caps with scrambled egg on their peaks!

The driver started the engine, and we two flung open the side doors, lifted the lids of our seats, grabbed the hose nozzles of both foam hoses and ran forward as if to simulate attacking a fire. This was where our bad fairy took a hand; not one, but both hoses jammed in their storage boxes after ten or twenty feet had run out, and what really caused the chaos was that our driver failed to note this. Actually, of course, this was as far as the demo should have proceeded, but there was almost as much froth and bubble in the driver's head as foam in the tank. A combination of a warm day, beer fumes, and the semi-paralysing presence of brass-hats persuaded him to engage the foam pump as if at a real fire and the results were nightmarish.

With no outlet to the hoses we held, the full pressure from the pump split one of the hoses in its box and pushed the other out in a parabolic curve inside the cab. This so disconcerted our poor driver that he failed to shut off immediately, and the whole vehicle was filled with foam. Why the three of us didn't spend the night in the guard-room, I'll never understand; perhaps they thought we were punished enough by having to clean up the vehicle - and ourselves - or, more likely, no one noticed that our performance was not due solely to being unfamiliar with the operation of a new type of fire-tender, or we should not have been allowed to drive back to Doni B in it.

One really intriguing problem that Jim Greenwood and I met that summer, was when we fitted a Koffman starter to one of the Swordfish. These starters were later used very effectively on the Merlins of Spitfire and Hurricane aircraft, and operated by using the explosive expansion of gases from a cartridge similar to, but larger than, a twelve-bore shot-gun cartridge.

The gases, in expanding, acted upon a device attached to the auxiliary drive-shaft of the engine, which then revolved the crankshaft sufficiently fast to start the engine. Our Swordfish were fitted with inertia-starters which were hand-wound by groundstaff using handles on either side of the nacelle. It would have been possible to fit electric starters, but on a flight deck the necessary battery trolleys would have been a dangerous encumbrance, and anyway, the Navy never used mechanical power if the job could be done by hand! The Koffman starter offered a good alternative and with its magazine of five cartridges seemed just the job.

However, events were to prove otherwise, for after fitting the gear we made an attempt to start her. There was a loud bang and a cloud of smoke from the starter gadget's exhaust, the Pegasus fired once and died on us; not to be deterred, we tried again, and again, but with no signs of further life from the Peggy. Checking over the engine at leisure - we checked everything possible - we discovered that the ignition timing was faulty. So, we retimed the magnetos, loaded up with fresh cartridges and tried again. The same result, a bang from the starter exhaust, one single firing from the Pegasus and dead silence. Checked, timing out again; why? The auxiliary drive-train of gears in a Pegasus was positive, a tubular steel drive-shaft splined into the rear of the crankshaft, all the gear drive to the mags was positive - no clutch like the supercharger drive. It was impossible for slip to occur. AH! The drive-shaft is twisted by the sudden torque, check that. Easier said than done, this, but we stripped it out and tested it for distortion. Absolutely nothing showed, except that three oil holes passing radially through to the centre of the tubular shaft were not in line, and there was no apparent reason why they should have been designed that way. Putting our technical reputations at some risk, we ordered a new shaft with fingers crossed. When it came, the oil holes WERE in line, so we didn't end up on the scaffold - but Peggies were not then or thereafter ever fitted with Koffman starters.

Most of that summer passed fairly uneventfully. The flying programme included practising deck-landings on a part of the 'drome which was marked out to simulate the flight-deck of FURIOUS. We of HQ Flight had little to do with these interesting procedures as we were employed in a similar manner to a station workshop section; engine changes and various repairs and experiments etc. Our most frequent view of the 'drome was during pre-breakfast PT.

One of my new 'shipmates', Don Roy, was a golfer who had his clubs with him at Donibristle. When I returned from a home leave in late July, I brought my clubs back with me, and thereafter we spent a great deal of our leisure time together sampling the courses within striking distance. We joined a beautifully laid-out club course on the shore of the Forth at Aberdour, and played often at Ferry Hills which was near the northern end of the Forth Bridge. We even went to Edinburgh and played the two municipal Braids Courses. Sixpence a round they charged there then! I wonder what the fees are today. Don was a good player - which wasn't surprising as his father was secretary of the club at Dun Laoghaire, near Dublin. After I'd left Doni B I didn't meet Don again until one day in the spring of 1940 he stepped out of a Blenheim which had called for re-fuelling at Nantes, en route to a bombing practice camp at Perpignan. I hope he survived, but the life-expectancy of Blenheim crews was not great in subsequent years.

On a more cheerful memory, '38 was the year that the Empire Exhibition was held at Glasgow, in fact I think it must have been the last time it was held anywhere. Despite the fellowship which brought people from all parts of the world to help Britain during 1939-45, the post-War years have seen the not-too-gradual dismantling of a Pax Britannica which covered about a third of the world.

Someone - there's always an organiser in even small groups - laid on a coach, and about a couple of dozen of us went over to Glasgow for a day at this Exhibition. Sitting next to me in the coach was Alwyn Monk, usually known by the Spoonerised nickname of Maffy Tonk. He and I had a little competition each day to see who could finish the Telegraph crossword first; on this day he gave forth to more than crosswords. It was a warmish day and during the journey he complained of being too warm. When I suggested that he put his macintosh over the back of the seat in front of us he did so - and disclosed the fact that the lighted end of a cigarette had lodged on his lap beneath the coat and was smouldering gently away at the front of his trousers. Most of the rest of that day he spent holding his mac in front of the largish hole.

The pavilions from the various Dominions and Colonies were quite spectacular, and I particularly remember the Canadian Mounties and the South Sea Islanders with their vicious-looking weapons made from frontal bones of swordfish and sawfish. Of course, there was a bar or two there, and on a hot day, where else would erks gravitate to? A good dozen of us put a couple of tables together and in the course of time, were singing the usual - and some unusual - service songs. We had one of our own which bears remembering, sung to the tune of Lily of Laguna:

'We are Furious,
We are so long and so curious,
Here we lie, at anchor all the day,
Waiting for the signal from the RFA.
We range up aircraft, in the morning
And we strike down in the evening;
There'll be no flying for today.'

Not exactly operatic class, but our own, and at least it was clean!

One day in September, the corporal of the fire-engine fiasco had the misfortune to depart from this life; I never found out how or why. He was a long-serving member of the personnel at Donibristle, with a family of quite numerous children, and it was the usual practice in such cases to have a good whip round. On this occasion, the CO decided that a dance should be held on the Camp with the proceeds to be given to the corporal's wife.

Jim Greenwood and myself were not dancing fanatics; it was some years later that I realised that I'd not meet many nice girls unless I <u>could</u> dance, and took lessons, so we two went for our usual walk down to St. David's Bay and the Fordell Arms. Getting back to Camp around 11.30 p.m., we crawled into our beds and were well away when there was a bit of a commotion; the lights came on in the billet, and there was our sergeant, shouting, "Come on, lads! Get dressed as quick as you can! Pack up your kit and get down to the workshop! War has been declared and we've to get our tools and spare engines down to Rosyth by dawn; the FURIOUS is in the Forth waiting for us!"

CHAPTER 10
At Scapa Flow

Neither Jim nor myself were in either a good mood or fit condition after such a rude awakening, but we were not alone in being rather less than enthusiastic, for the tasks which we were called upon during the next few hours - many of the dancing fraternity were also slightly incapacitated by their evening's entertainment. Nevertheless, when the grey light of dawn broke we were all ready to leave Doni B.

Our personal kits were packed and parked; the two spare Pegasus and the spare Kestrel were recrated, all tools and equipment which didn't belong to Donibristle were packed, and most of it was loaded onto station transport. It only remained to get it and ourselves down to the dockyard at Rosyth.

And there, lying against the loading jetty, was a surprise - to me at least. An old friend was going to ferry us and our kit across to FURIOUS which was sitting off the dockyard in the centre of the Forth; it was the drifter 'Noontide', she must have sailed up from Plymouth ahead of the carrier but her top speed couldn't have been more than about eight knots.

All our gear had now to be hoisted from the road transport, on to the small deck of 'Noontide', and from there, using one of the two derrick cranes on FURIOUS's quarterdeck, inboard, and right through the lower hanger to forward of the forward lift-well. Sounds complicated and long-winded, but it took remarkably little time; there was an urgency in everything we did by this stage. There's an old saying, 'needs must when the devil drives'. Whatever was driving us, whether it was Chiefy or our own sense of the importance and excitement of the moment, by 0700 hours we were steaming out under that engineering marvel, the Forth Bridge.

Accompanying us were not only our usual consort, the destroyer, HMS Keith, but a county class cruiser, HMS Cornwall - and three other destroyers. This formidable group of warships was, according to a knowledgeable matelot, our full War complement - it seemed true then that we were actually at war! We were finally fully convinced when we discovered that the ship was full of reservists, who had been recalled to the Service at what they described as a moment's notice.

These ancient mariners were finding life pretty crowded, as indeed were the rest of the regular crew, and were having to sling their hammocks anywhere they could find space, or just spread them on the hangar deck.

Most of my fellow erks in HQ Flight had not been in FURIOUS before; Maffy Tonk had, and there was a corporal fabric-worker, Sam Sugarman, who'd been with her when she'd called at Gibraltar before my time. The last time FURIOUS had served with the Mediterranean Fleet was in 1935, but a quick run to Gib., could take under three days when she picked up her skirts.

And the old flat top was doing just that as we sailed northwards up the coast of Scotland, flying-on the Swordfish and Ospreys of our three Flights. Perhaps I should call them Squadrons as the Navy was tending to do when taking over matters pertaining to flying, where ships were also concerned. The Admiralty probably never forgave the Air Ministry for taking the Royal Naval Air Service from them when the RAF was formed in 1918; and the subsequent record of the Fleet Air Arm during the '39-45 fun and games showed that they may have had a point.

There was much to do once we had found somewhere to park our kit and ourselves. Finding one's way around the ship was fairly long-term even when, as in my own case, there was always some old salt to ask, but most of the present RAF contingent hadn't even seen FURIOUS before their first sight that dawn. There were, as said before, several who had been in FURIOUS before and a few more who had been in other carriers or served in those light cruisers which carried float planes or even Walruses (Walri?). This need to know the ropes as soon as possible after joining obviously had a bearing on the RAF's policy of repeat postings of personnel with previous experience of the Fleet Air Arm.

One job that our fitter sergeant decided we should do at an early opportunity was to unpack the workshop toolkit we had been issued with for Kestrel engines. When we gathered it all in our little workshop there was very little room for us as well; we calculated that it must have cost at least as much as an engine complete. Its cases were made of solid teak, with carrying handles outside, and inside every tool was ensconced in shaped nests which were also of teak - real teak, that is, not the modern day teak-veneered chipboard.

Unfortunately, the cases were also filled with packing, although there was no great need of this to our minds. The packing consisted of large amounts of coloured paper strips, like the streamers one used to throw about at parties; a waste product of some process of course, and a damn nuisance to us at that time.

A solution occurred to me - the gash-chute on the bulwark by the ship's galley was fitted and its water lubrication system in operation. "That'll do," I thought, and suiting the action to the thought, gathered up a great armful of the stuff and stepped out of the workshop with it. As I walked along the side deck towards the gash-chute I lost a few streamers of paper; at least I thought it was few, but with the ship doing about twenty-five knots or so, the draught was considerably faster than my walk speed. As I reached the chute and stuffed my load into it I realised - too late - that the air was full of paper packing streamers blowing away along the side of the ship towards the quarter-deck. Absolute panic set in, I dashed smartly back to the workshop and tried to get most of the rest of the rubbish back into a case and out of sight before Nemesis overtook in the form of the Officer of the Watch. We did manage it, and also managed to rid ourselves of the rest of the packing in rather smaller quantities.

We never did find out just what the Navy thought of their decorated ship and I, at least, was quite happy to hear no more.

This cruise, or whatever it would eventually be called, was not going to be the best of voyages for our Naval hosts nor yet for we 'crab-fat matelots' as they often called us. Having used this epithet, a little explanation might be in order here. In all three Services the usual treatment used against body-lice - which were called 'crabs' in the vernacular - was a mercury-based ointment which was of a similar colour to our Air Force blue uniforms. Even this disparaging description was preferable to being called Brylcreem Boys because of some damned advertisement.

One day during the dash northward, we had an occasion to test run the engine of one of the Swordfish after some work had been carried out on it. This entailed taking the aircraft up on the flight deck by means of the forward lift.

The top surface of the lift was flush with the flight deck and when in its lower positions, flush with both lower hangar and upper hangar decks; when at sea it was mostly at its upper point, but in harbour if not actually raining, we left it level with the lower hanger deck and used daylight to work by. If we happened to be up top when breaktime was piped, it was customary - but officially frowned upon - to slide down one or other of the H section girders which acted as guides for the lift, using hands and shoe insteps as brakes: bad for the condition of overall fronts, but great fun.

When running engines on the flight deck it was usual to take some precautions against fire, so we took a couple of extinguishers and the wheel chocks up with us. As the Pegasus had not been run for a day or so, the fitter in the office gave it a little fuel-priming with the KI-gas pump. Perhaps a few too many pumps because it dripped from the carburettor air intake and formed a little pool on the deck beneath. That would not have mattered much but when she fired there was a flame blow-back which ignited both the intake and, by a burning drip, the pool on the deck. Not to be found wanting in an emergency, yours truly smacked the knob of one of the foam extinguishers and promptly stopped further conflagration. There's a lot of foam in one of those extinguishers and once set off they carry on until empty. The flight deck was of course, of steel plate, the steel plates were covered by timbers and the timber was finished off with granulated cork admixed with an asphaltic substance, to offer a grip to the tyres of aircraft when landing-on. Once again, I found that this is an unjust world; instead of being congratulated for my prompt action, I found myself lumbered with the task of scrubbing foam from the interstices between cork particles.

Sometime during that run, one of our spare cased Peggies which were 'stored' in what we were wont to describe as Aircraft Repair Section - that is, the section of the lower hangar forward of the lift-well - broke loose. As the ship rolled and pitched, so it was dancing to and fro, to the general detriment. It wasn't going to damage the ship much, but having taken a life of its own, it seemed determined to damage both itself and its two fellow spare engines. As we landlubbers took ropes and our lives in our hands to restrain this one-ton cube, it looked likely to damage us too! However, by means of some lively side-stepping and cowboy-style rope casting, we did manage to get it tied down and once more immobile.

By the time that we had all settled in and considered ourselves to be seasoned sailors of several days, our small fleet of ships arrived at what appeared to be a completely landlocked sea; this we discovered to be the fabulous Scapa Flow, the impregnable haven of the Home

Fleet, and scene of the scuttling of the German Grand Fleet after their surrender in 1918. At one point of the voyage we had had a slight encounter with Encounter[1], but life had been so hectic and new to most of us that it had passed practically unnoticed; an aircraft carrier is so large that perhaps it might sink and not be noticed until one's feet got wet!

The sights that met our eyes on all quarters in that landlocked sea area were tremendously exciting, and filled me with pride to think that I was a part of it all. In every direction in which one looked could be seen ships which were well-known by name but not too often seen, and certainly not gathered together in one great fleet. From memory, there was Warspite, Ramilles and Hood, with attendant destroyers, and several county class cruisers; there was our sister carrier, Courageous, and one or two subs among the many vessels present.

All told, there must have been forty-odd warships, and to cap it, one morning what should appear on the near horizon but Repulse and Renown in their light grey Mediterranean livery.

Despite the mass of shipping, there was still room for both us and the Courageous to range-up and fly-off aircraft, although this did entail our sailing in a great circle, one behind the other.

It was during this flying programme that we had the only accident on deck which I witnessed.

There were, if I remember correctly, four or five arrestor wires fitted athwartships, to assist in keeping landing kites on the island, by catching the arrestor hooks fitted to the undersides of their fuselages. These wires were lifted to about two feet above the deck by hinged arms which fell back to the deck when an aircraft hooked onto a wire. The wires ran from these arms to large drums situated below the flight deck, in the upper hangar; drums which were fitted with hydraulic damping to slow down the landing speed of an aircraft fairly drastically. If one were in the upper hangar when an aircraft landed-on, the crashing down of the arms onto the deck and the whirl of the drums made one think that the kite had crashed when first hearing it.

On this one and only occasion which I saw, an Osprey came in a little high and missed all the wires. Instead of opening up and attempting to take off again, the aircraft swung to starboard and hit the navigator's bridge before taking a dive over the side.

---

[1]H.M.S. Encounter was a destroyer.

The officer who was conning the ship, and his attendant ratings were lucky to escape decapitation even though these port and starboard bridges were hydraulically lowered during flying.

These Ospreys had a dinghy stored in the centre section of the upper mainplane, which was attached to the aircraft by a steel cable from its underside. When operated by the crew, a gas bottle inflated the dinghy with sufficient force to burst the linen covering of its stowage. This was, on first acquaintance, an excellent method of preventing the aircraft from descending rapidly to the seabed, and thus saving tax-payers' money. The powers that be had not yet reached the stage obtaining later, when lives and materials would be sacrificed on the altar of the politically expedient advantage of giving the enemy a bloody nose and our politicians an accolade!

Just how it was accomplished probably even the pilot didn't know, but he succeeded in releasing the dinghy between hitting the bridge and hitting the sea! And not only that, but both he and his TAG crew were in that dinghy almost before it hit the water!

As we were sailing at thirty-ish knots it became our destroyer Keith's task to collect the crew and salvage the Osprey. It was easy to pick up the crew and they soon had the kite, still attached to its dinghy, drawn up alongside, if a little wet! By this time the two ships were hove-to about two hundred yards apart. It was decided to take a line over to Keith, attach it to the aircraft, and bring it over to us to lift it from the sea, using one of the derricks on our quaterpatch.

That seemed the obvious method from our end of the line which had been taken across to HMS Keith; but then we didn't know that they had disconnected the Osprey from its dinghy when they had salvaged it and tied it up alongside, tail up like a stranded whale. As our destroyer escort lived up to its name and released the aircraft to be drawn across to us, it did what most metal objects do in water and sank beneath the surface. Had the water in Scapa Flow been deeper than the tow line was long, everything would have gone more or less according to plan; but it was not! The poor old Osprey sank to the bottom, and when our derrick drew in the tow-line, it was dragged along there, disturbing all the bottom-feeding aquatic life and lots of mud. The consequence was, naturally, that when it was drawn from the hoggin and lowered to the immaculately scrubbed oaken planks of the quarterdeck, it brought with it a goodly sample of the sea-bottom. Add that to a considerable leakage of oil from the oil-tank and engine breathers, coolant from the radiator and 87 octane petrol, the state of mind of the First Lieutenant and his minions can be easily appreciated.

Their first instinctive reaction must have been to cast the lot back over the side, but they perhaps thought that the damage now having been done, we may as well continue the salvage operation. The airframe was considerably the worse for wear after its two hundred yard slide across the seafloor, so it was decided perforce, that only the engine and items which remained relatively undamaged should be saved. The big item was the engine so we fetched our Ern-Lake type engine stand and set about freeing the Kestrel from the tangle of airframe tubes, pipe lines, and wiring. When we had finally bolted the engine onto the stand, the remainder of the airframe was in an even sorrier state than before; it was doubtless with great relief that the Navy lifted the dripping mess with the derrick and disposed of it with a welcome splash over the side. All they had to contend with now was a large area of mud, oil and sundry wildlife, a series of grooves cut into their beautiful planking by the engine stand and the greasy footprints of some four or five disgustingly irreverent erks.

Our work also was not by any means ended. We now had to strip the Kestrel completely in order to salvage as many of its component parts as we could. Seawater has a most derogatory effect, on aluminium alloys particularly and does nothing good to steel and copper-based alloys; so speed of action was going to be imperative.

In our little workshop there were of course, paraffin baths for cleaning engine parts, but here in FURIOUS, we also had a bath in which we could run water and heat the water with a steam pipe. One thing about living in a naval sea-going environment was that there was seldom a lack of heating: but quite the reverse when in dry dock.

As each part was removed from the Kestrel, so it was boiled in this bath before drying roughly and following on with a wash in paraffin and final oil coating before storing prior to examination in detail. Sounds a bit complicated, and so it was. The workshop toolkit which we had only so recently unpacked really came into its own during these twenty-four or so hours, which it took us to reduce a complete engine to its separate components. As fast as we undoubtedly worked, we were not quick enough to save much of the light alloy parts from the effects of salt attack. In particular, I recall that when we parted the supercharger housing, where the casing had been in close proximity to the stainless steel blades of the impeller fan, it was quite deeply eaten away; probably an electrolytic action between the dissimilar metals

There was no ceasing of work on this engine until it was indeed finished; we had breaks for meals naturally and took a breather on the gun sponson just outside our workshop occasionally, but that was all. It never failed to surprise me just what can be accomplished when people really put their minds to it and get involved. During the real enthusiasm of the task it's not very extraordinary that the deck became almost a skating rink with oil from the parts being carried around, and steam from the water bath condensing over all, so sawdust was added copiously to the mix.

The bulkheads were actually running with water - and some of it could have been our sweat! For it was very warm during that hectic day and night - but when we cleaned up the workshop afterwards the steel plates of the deck looked like polished mirrors. Now this was really remarkable - and welcome - it is Naval tradition that every Saturday morning the Captain has 'Rounds'; he inspects every part of his command, in the company of the Officer of the Watch, and sundry others such as the disciplinary Warrant Officer, or 'Jaunty'. In order to give this invasion the impression that polishing and painting were all we did or wanted to do, it had been the practice to polish the deck with a revolting mixture of paraffin and powdered graphite. This in a part of the ship where several of us actually LIVED; if one was careless enough to drop one's towel or an item of kit on this deck, it took on the appearance of oily rags.

The effect tended to wear off during the week, so that by Friday most of the mess had been transferred either to our clothing or to the nice wooden deck surrounding our No. 1 gun during smoking times.

It so happened that I knew that we only had three pounds of graphite powder remaining in the stores, and this was packed in bags made of the same thick blue paper, which even today is known as sugar-paper. This knowledge gave me the bright idea that if all that graphite disappeared we should be able to retain our nice clean deck for the remainder of the cruise. Picking a time when the workshop and store were vacant, I nipped into the stores, collared the three bags and dumped them smartly over the side. Perhaps the reader wonders just what we needed graphite for anyway. It was mixed with light grease and when sparking plugs were fitted, the threads were smeared with the mixture. As the grease burned off, the graphite remained to lubricate the threads, so making it much easier to remove the plugs and obviating the possibility of seizure. All would have been well, had we been under way, but we had been anchored by our front end since the accident. Most of the ships around us were also at anchor; the ship just swung around with the action of any wind - or tide - and always pointed into wind; this meant that the view from our messdeck and workshop changed with the wind.

Just forward of our sponson there was a boom which was rigged to jut out at right angles to the ship's side, and to which were tethered any of the ship's boats which were not inboard on their davits. At this time there were two there, attached by their painters to the beam. When the boat's crew went aboard their craft, they had to walk along the beam and down a rope ladder to the boat. Over the side of the quarterdeck there was rigged a proper stairway, which the Navy probably called a ladder, and the boats were taken there by their crews to pick up or disembark passengers; including of course airmen and naval enlisted men. One of the boats tied up to the beam was the Captain's launch, a lovely white-enamelled power boat, all polished brass and scrubbed white canvas; the other was one of the boats used for liberty boats, grey-painted, fairly open hull with two canvas-covered hoods as protection for the occupants.

Some hours after I'd disposed so neatly - I thought - of the three packs, I heard a commotion over the side, and looking down saw that the pair of boats alongside were looking more than a little the worse for being streaked with some black substance which appeared to cover the surface of the sea in our vicinity. There was evidently not a great 'wet-strength' in sugar-paper. There must however, have been strength in the arms of my guardian angel, for as far I could ascertain, no-one connected this tragedy with the continued polish of our workshop deck.

There were, I fear, a few quizzical looks around us from our sergeant, who must have missed the presence of the bags of graphite from shelves in what amounted to his cabin, but even he must also have seen that the deck was so much better to live with than before. Nothing was actually said or done about the matter; except, no doubt by the crews of the affected boats on the boom!

The news gradually filtered down to us that we were not actually at war with anyone - yet - that the whole episode had been in the nature of an exercise on the one hand, and on another had been carried out as some manner of backup for our prime minister, Mr. Chamberlain, as he tried to frighten Hitler from his proposed taking over of Czechoslovakia. History tells us that although he thought he had succeeded, events proved it a hollow success, but whatever was to happen in the future, for the present, the Fleets began to disperse from Scapa Flow, and FURIOUS was to return to Rosyth, so that our excessive complement of reservists could be disembarked and sent home to their loving families.

It was with mixed feelings that this news was greeted, to balance against the return to RAF rations, were the prospects of golf with Don and more of that reasonably good Scots beer. Most of this latter was bottled and known as either light or heavy 'dumps'; perhaps it was brewed in Dunfermline, I never discovered why. Speaking of beer, there was a peculiar law in Scotland at that time; the pubs shut all day on Sundays, except for what were called *bona fide* travellers. In practice, if one wanted a drink, one signed the visitors' book, stating origin and proposed destination therein. Some very interesting journeys were recorded; and some all-night sessions occurred occasionally, when bars closed at 11.30 Saturday, to open again at 00.01 on Sunday morning!

As we sailed past the small island of Inchkeith in the mouth of the Forth, we were paraded on the foredeck. This was generally known as the fore-flying-off deck because in past years aircraft had been flown straight out of the lower hangar doors - a reason I always found hard to believe - and it was most certainly not possible in 1938 with all those anti-aircraft guns emplaced on it. There was plenty of room however, for HQ to have our morning parade there, with a last post-breakfast smoke before turning in to the workshop.

On this occasion, however, we were there for a different reason, and also accompanied by some deck-hand matelots and marines. We were there to 'assist' the First Lieutenant, who, incidentally was a Commander by rank and usually known as Jimmy the One, the man in fact who really ran the ship just as in the RAF and the Army, the adjutant ran the Unit for the C.O.

This time we were not going to just drop the hook, but were going to tie up to a buoy opposite Rosyth Dockyard, sailing under the Forth Bridge to do so.

Sounds simple, but nothing is or was simple in Nelson's Navy. One of the ship's boats was launched as we sailed slower and slower up the river; not one of the powered ones, this was special, with about a dozen oarsmen and a coxswain. A light line was passed down the ship through a fairlead on the starboard side in the bows, to the seaboat which was some distance aft. This line was followed by a grass rope of about two inches in diameter, and then, we assembled mixture of odds and sods were formed into a continuous line along the fore-flying-off deck to draw the grass through the fairlead and thus aid the rowers to keep up with the ship. As each man reached the aft end of the deck near the forward hangar doors, he had to double back to the stem to take a fresh grip of the grass as it came inboard.

The object of this complicated manoeuvre was for Jimmy to so gauge things that FURIOUS's bows, and her grass-drawn seaboat arrived at the appropriate buoy simultaneously, so that the boat's crew could then tie us up neatly to the buoy - just as FURIOUS lost all forward way. Not easy!

The conductor of this magnum opus was standing in the Navigator's Bridge - the same starboard one which the Osprey had attempted to wreck - with a loud-hailer to direct both us and the seaboat's crew. All was going well, most of the directives which we received were of the "Haul away, handsomely," type and easily understood, but when the action became more delicate and crucial, just as the seaboat reached within a couple of feet of the buoy, there was a bellow of "Avast heaving," from above. Now any matelot knows that that means "Stop pulling," but it was Jimmy's bad luck that at that critical moment, the grass was being manned almost exclusively by RAF bods who were, for the most part ignorant of such finer nuances of English - and took it that they were to "Fast Heave." We did just that, and the consequences were disastrous. Fifty or so men can exert quite a pull on a rope and we brought the bows of the rowing boat out of the water to such an angle that the unfortunate crew were cast into the hoggin, and unable to hook up to the buoy. Of course, they weren't drowned and did manage to rescue their oars and the situation, but that Commander must have been very glad when the Navy finally ridded itself of those grey-blue clad menaces to good order.

But it was not to be for some time yet, although there was a general "buzz" that it was the RAF's intention to pass over all sea-going air activities to the Beef and Gravy, and also possibly, Coastal Command duties.

Nothing really noteworthy happened that I recall, whilst we were still aboard FURIOUS in the Forth; I do remember with some distaste, missing the last liberty boat from South Queensferry after an autumn evening in Edinburgh, and then having to wait for the first morning boat - around 7 a.m. - an unforgettably miserable night that was.

However, it was not long before HQ Flight was back ashore at Doni B, where one of the first jobs we had was in giving a similar treatment to a Pegasus which the Kestrel from the Osprey had received at Scapa Flow. The Swordfish from which it was removed had not in this instance gone over the side of the ship, but had made a forced landing. The pilot had thought he was lucky, when engine trouble had made a landing imperative, in spotting a nice long level area along the south coast of the Forth somewhere to the east of Leith. Level it may have been, but it was also soft, deep mud, and offered a far greater resistance to forward motion than the carrier's arrestor wires.

Who the lucky lads were who had had the sticky job of salvaging the remains, I don't know, but the Peggie ended up in our ERS at Donibristle for the attempt to rescue parts before saltwater ruined them: the usual all-night session was then preceded and followed by a normal day's work. Most of us actually enjoyed these extensions of demand on our powers of endurance and sense of humour and they were, indeed, useful training for what was to come in the not too distant future.

Only a few weeks remained of 1938, and it passed unremarkably except for plenty of golf with Don Roy and ditto of beer with Jim Greenwood and others. Having had an interest in RAF power boats aroused by working on the Napier Lion engine belonging to the Boat section at Rosyth, I tried to remuster to the trade of Fitter, Driver

Petrol, Marine, when a notice was promulgated at Doni asking for volunteers, to be informed that there was no chance for me as it only applied to RAF personnel in the UK, and I was in the FAA and regarded as being overseas!

It was shortly after this disappointment, that I learned that I was to be relieved by a naval rating, and as it was near Christmas and I had a couple of weeks' leave due to me, I applied for it to coincide with my posting. This was OK'd and off I went - with some regret I may add - on two weeks' leave with a rail-warrant from Donibristle to Henlow in Bedfordshire, routed through the old home town.

CHAPTER 11
Henlow and War Preparations

Arriving at Henlow was a bit like having a cold bath on a midsummer day - something of a shock to the system. Some RAF stations were cosy places, small huts, the inhabitants of which were akin to a family, others were of the Uxbridge depot type, large barrack blocks of two or more stories - Henlow was of the latter type. There are or were, advantages of course: the water in what were known as the ablutions was usually hot, the NAAFI was large enough to employ several young ladies to serve 'tea and a wad' at break time, and suppers and beers in the 'wet' canteen during the evening.

Henlow was a well established place with its own railway terminus, and what seemed like acres of factory-like buildings. It was in one of these large empty warehouses that the unit to which I had been posted was to form a new and major engine repair depot. The nucleus of this unit was being staffed by REAL old sweats of the kind who hithertofore I had looked upon with some awe. Of the fifty or so who arrived there in the first week or so of 1939, every one was only recently back in Blighty after overseas service. There were men fresh from five years in India, Iraq, Egypt and Aden. Some from long service in Malaya, Singapore, the two stations in China, Hong Kong and Shanghai - there probably was no overseas unit not represented among us, and not to forget those who had been guests of the RN in the various carriers around the world, and in cruisers which carried Ospreys or Walruses. A motley bunch indeed, and I was one of them.

Before very long I was joined at Henlow by Maffy Tonk and one of the Orderly Room clerks from FURIOUS, a young lad we used to call Daphne to tease him because of his good looks - quite unjustified slander I fear. The Navy must have decommissioned the ship early so that she could go into dock again for a few 'slight' alterations; like changing her 5.5 guns for a dozen 4 inch HA/LA anti aircraft guns, and fitting her with a superstructure to the side of the flight-deck! She must have ended up looking just like any other common or garden carrier!

Coming back to my new station, the situation was fairly fluid for some time, so your scribe gave himself the job of more or less permanent room orderly; a task which entailed making sure the room was tidy, floor shining brightly, washbowls, baths etc., gleaming, and nothing where it shouldn't be. By morning break this task would normally be completed and the duty orderly would proceed to his place of work. As there seemed no great urgency I did this orderly for several weeks and never showed my face at the workshop, until one day a fellow told me, "You're wanted. The Warrant Officer wants you in the office straight away." I knew the WO in question from my arrival, and he looked to me a fairly ferocious type. He had retired from the RAF once on a pension, and taken the tenancy of the pub not far from the camp gates, but had been recalled from the Reserve.

As the message seemed rather urgent, I just slipped on my tunic and dashed along to the workshop office.

"You sent for me, Sir?"

"Did I? Who are you, then? And what the devil is that sticking out of your collar?"

In my haste I had left the collar of a khaki woollen overseas-type shirt to show above the old button-up type tunic I was wearing - most untidy - as I was then told in no uncertain terms.

That was the end of the room orderly skive, I fear; from then on, I was kept reasonably busy. The work at this time was fitting work benches with steel sheet work surfaces, soldering over the screwheads which held down the steel, then fitting vices to the benches and arranging the benches to form bays. This took quite some time; it was going to be a very large undertaking, but eventually engines did begin to arrive. The system was to completely dismantle engines, to clean all parts, in similar fashion to that used at Donibristle and at Scapa Flow, and then inspect for possible re-use or scrapping, before storing in the appropriate bay for reassembly. One difference was that we used a steam-heated bath of trichloroethylene instead of just water as in Scotland. This led to an unfortunate accident when a corporal, who was cleaning one of these tanks, was rendered unconscious by the fumes - dodgy stuff is trike!

One of the large buildings at Henlow was occupied by the parachute packing unit. Some stations had their own parachute section with the necessary long polished-top table, but Henlow was the central depot for all other units. The 'chutes were tested on a sample basis, and this was done from a Vickers Virginia. There was a catwalk affair fitted to the lower mainplane and the tester walked along this to the end of the wing - holding on to a safety rail, of course - and just pulled the rip-cord. The opening of the 'chute took over from then; there was no chance of a change of mind. Most of this testing was done by volunteers, and I've often since regretted not having had a bash.

Henlow being within easy reach of the Smoke, I managed a couple of weekends there at the Union Jack Club, one of which was spent with Bert Jones, whom I'd last seen before he was posted to the Glorious in the Med. He was living up to his goal of Sergeant Pilot, for he had managed to get his 'props', i.e. had been promoted to Leading Aircraftman, and this, with his remustering to Group One trade, had qualified him for aircrew. I knew from his letters that he'd been back in the UK at an initial flying training school, but by now he was fitted with wings and training on single-seaters. A public school education in the art of rugby playing had really paid dividends!

One other trip to London was when a group of us, including Taff and Daphne, decided to attend a rugby match between England and Wales. For various reasons, as will transpire, we never actually arrived at Twickenham. What does remain as a memory of that trip was when we became inadvertently embroiled in a battle between a bunch of queers and a group of prostitutes - all we wanted was a few pints in that pub somewhere along Tottenham Court Road - where even the bar tables were flying around, never mind the bottles and glasses, before we managed to get clear from the scene of conflict.

The day did nearly end in tragedy, for Daphne dropped his Underground ticket as we waited for our train at Goodge Street, and when it fluttered down between the rails, jumped down to retrieve it. The rails there were raised on insulated posts about a foot above the track base, but he must have had his personal guardian angel present, it was only when he regained the platform and we unkindly told him our opinion of him that he realised what he had done and fainted on us!

Because Taffy lived in that far-off country beyond Wales - Pembroke Dock - when we were granted five days' leave at Easter, I invited him to my home in Wolves, and neither of us stepped out of the straight and narrow during the whole weekend, such was the power of parental discipline in those days.

It was just as well that I took that Easter break, because there was no further leave coming my way that year. Henlow being a non-operational station, it more or less closed down for a fixed leave period in the manner of many civilian factories. Naturally, SOME bods had to remain in camp to maintain security and the essential services. Other things being equal, it's always a good idea to be on what are really special assignments, so I volunteered to be one of the maintenance party, for guard duties, fire pickets, etc...

One day, soon after the main body of troops had departed on leave, a group of us were sitting in our barrack-room playing cards, when who should walk in but my 'friend' the WO.

"I see you're all very busy, I'll not keep you long, I just want one volunteer for a special job."

Well, I thought, I owe you one for not having me shot, so I did what tradition says should never be done, and said, "Will I do, Sir?"

"You'll do fine, lad. See me right after breakfast tomorrow, and have your small kit with you."

When I obeyed this instruction, I was presented with a rail-warrant and instructions to report to No. 43 Squadron at Tangmere, and to bloody-well BEHAVE myself. What could be better, I thought, a holiday by the seaside and all paid for by the RAF? And so it, more or less, turned out to be.

On arrival at Tangmere, I was allocated a bunk and told to report to the technical Flight Sergeant of one of the Squadron's three Flights; I forget which it was now, and that's not surprising as will be apparent as this account unfolds. The Chiefy I reported to was a bit dumbfounded by my arrival and his reaction was, "What the hell am I going to do with you? I've more bods than I know what to do with already! The best thing you can do is go and get lost somewhere. There's Bognor Regis, just down the road, and you can alternate that with Chichester."

Being, as I was, a fairly adept column-dodger by now, I didn't need being told, and took myself off happily.

The official reason for my being attached to this crack fighter squadron, was that the RAF - and possibly the other two Services - were having one of those mock war exercises where Red forces were arranged against Blue forces; in this instance, Tangmere was being defended against invading forces. Never believe that good old England was not prepared for war in '39 - or even '38; although we could have been BETTER prepared, certainly with more efficient and modern aircraft. The aircrew and technical maintenance personnel

Fig. 1　　Group of recruit squad, under training at Uxbridge. (Top row: l to r) Ludlow, Bill Eddy, Pat Kavanagh, Alf Shrabsole, Bob, G G Jones, Dixie. (Middle row: l to r) unknown, Reg Batcher, Nat Chinnock, Moss, (Bottom row: l to r) Derek Linley, Gwynne Jones, Bill Bullock.

Fig. 2　　Aerial view of R.A.F. Manston

Fig. 3 Osprey in 'warpaint' and new type hangar at R.A.F. Thornaby, 1935

Fig. 4 Internal view of barrack-room, Thornaby

Fig. 5   An Audax and an ambulance meet!
(Described in Chapter 4)

Fig. 6   Views of R.A.F. Hullavington

Fig. 7   E.R.S. Furious

Fig. 8   H.M.S. Furious

Fig. 9   R.A.F. Donibristle, Fife

Fig. 10   The author and his Raleigh M/C

Fig. 11   A cushy billet at Blickling Hall

Fig. 12   The crews of the last two Blenheims of 18 Sqdn. to leave Malta, including the author

Fig. 13   18 Sqdn. Ground Staff at Sidi Barrani, 1942

were as good as any in the world and much better than most. The ground staff were to form a solid nucleus for the rapid expansion to come, but many of our peace-time pilots and aircrew were to be wasted in the early months of what became known as the Phoney War by being sent into action in such sadly underperforming aircraft as Fairey Battles, A.W. Whitleys and Gladiators, which attractive as they may have looked to the brass-hats, were no match for our well-practised enemies, flying aeroplanes proven by action in earlier theatres.

But I digress too far and too early perhaps: war was certainly being prepared for at Tangmere. One day a Blenheim of the opposing force attacked us and a flour-bomb put paid to the NAAFI canteen, which effectively also put paid to sessions on the billiards tables for this skiving historian. Little remained after that in the way of entertainment on the station but cardplaying in the barrack-room but that was somewhat inhibited by the fact that black-out curtains were fitted to the windows, and these were of such complexity and difficulty in fitting that they were left in situ - to the great detriment of the atmosphere. Going out of camp was the only recourse left; and it was only the lack of money after about two weeks that decided me to seek out the Flight Sergeant in the hangar. His reaction to my appearance was a bit disconcerting.

"What! You still here? I thought you'd been gone last week! You'd better get up to the orderly-room and buzz off back to where you came from!"

There were no cans to carry when I returned to Henlow, unless one considers to be a retribution the fact that I found, on return to the fold, that all leave was cancelled. This was a bit of a disaster in itself, but there was worse to come.

Just lately, I had been spending almost as much time on other stations and in travel to and from them, as at Henlow. It had been only a couple of weeks before going to 43 Squadron at Tangmere that I had been sent down to West Drayton to take the trade test for promotion to Leading Aircraftman. No result, favourable or otherwise, had been given at the time, but I must have been successful, for my 'props' did eventually feed through the system later - with effect from November 1st!

During the next fortnight, there was much talk of a possibility of war with Germany over some dispute about Poland. Many of us took this with a pinch of salt. We'd heard rumours like this before, as witness the panic run up to Scapa Flow in the previous autumn, but this DID seem more serious, and when, one Sunday, we were told to assemble in the NAAFI *en masse*, that reinforced the serious aspect: to be ordered to go to the canteen was really unusual!

This, of course, was the occasion when Neville Chamberlain made the announcement that Germany had continued to attack Poland, and that we were now engaged for a second round of hostilities.

For some time now, there had been a modicum of interest aroused by the formation on the station of a new unit whose intended sphere of operation was indicated by its title, 21 Aircraft Depot, a unit which was destined to move elsewhere. With the PM's announcement, it became known that the destination was France. Probably because of my attachment to Tangmere, I was not on this draft, and because most of the bods of my present unit were, I was properly cheesed off about it.

However, it so happened that one who WAS on it told me that his exchange posting to the New Zealand Air Force had come through. It took a very short time for me to see my friendly enemy the WO engineer and point out to him that he'd now be a man short for his draft, and would I do?

"Just leave it to me," he said. I did, and he was as good as his word. For the next couple of weeks I was in a mood of excitement and suppressed energy. After that September 3rd, we were no longer permitted the privilege of wearing civilian clothes for what was euphemistically described as walking-out. In consequence, one evening when I strolled into my favourite pub, The Sun, in Hitchin, for a pint of their Worthington, I found that it was officers only, and out of bounds to other ranks! The WAR was certainly coming home to us now!

CHAPTER 12
B.E.F. Nantes and St. Nazaire

And that seemed to be the sum total result of being at war, no civvies, and restricted areas off camp as well as in camp; it looked as if the same old group were going to run this one that made such a mess of the '14-18 effort.

Nevertheless, by the 18th of September, we (21 AD that is) were ready for the off, and entrained for Southampton. There we went aboard what my faint memory recalls as a civilian ship, and four of us were ensconced in a four-berth cabin. A cabin without porthole, scuttle, or whatever from which we could monitor our condition and progress. Among four airmen, one was bound to possess a pack of cards, so we spent our waiting time sitting on the two bottom bunks playing solo whist. The ship at last began to vibrate as they do when moving, which went on for what seemed hours, perhaps forty-five minutes; then there was an almighty crash and we thought, "That's it. We've been torpedoed." Diving out of the cabin smartly, we learned that it was just the anchor being dropped off Spithead, while we waited for the convoy to assemble. Sheepishly creeping back to the cabin and our game, we were none of us really able to sleep much, and were glad when we arrived off Cherbourg just as daylight also arrived. From Cherbourg we entrained, and although the train was not exactly one of those used during the Great War, marked as fit for 8 chevaux/40 hommes, it was about six classes below LMS 3rd class standard. We were in that train for at least twenty-four hours, with stops for food, and other necessary bodily functions. One station sticks in the mind, Angers (where Cointreau is made); here the toilets were what would today be called unisex! There was the usual wall for males to stand against, and opposite was a row of compartments with half-doors, which we were surprised to note were used indiscriminately by male and female patrons.

The train eventually came to its destination sometime late on the afternoon following. We were then marched to a nearby aerodrome where an obviously newly built double hangar was seen. We marched into that hangar, and continued in our columns right round the inside of it to form a great circle, choking from the black dust which rose from the unfinished ash-strewn floor. While we stood there, gasping for breath and choking for a pint of good English ale, we were given a lecture by a Group Captain MacRae, on how to behave in a foreign country. We were told how the local wine would rot our socks, how the local lasses would perhaps rot some other parts, how we were to kip down just there in that hangar - all at least two hundred of us - until we could get tents erected, and, above all, we must fear God and honour the King. Honour the King we might, but it wasn't God we feared: it was people like him with their priorities just a bit out of kilter.

Eventually, after what seemed an age, but was probably not much more than a week, we had managed to install ourselves in a tented camp. This camp was situated in an orchard of apple and pear trees which had not been harvested that year. The Chateau Bougonne, of which the orchard was a part of the grounds, pretty obviously was not occupied and was fairly badly neglected. This was in all probability because of its proximity to the aerodrome: on the opposite side of which to the double hangar where we'd been accommodated, was an aircraft factory of some magnitude. This factory was part of France's nationalised aircraft industry and known as S.N.C.A.O. - Société Nationale Construction Aéronautique de l'Ouest, or something like that. More about them later perhaps.

The tents we were now to live in were ridge tents fourteen feet square, and we were given one between fourteen lads; heating, when the weather really deteriorated, was old oil drums, burning coke, outside the tents of course, and one fire between three tents. We didn't perspire much that winter of '39-40. Having the fire outside had its advantages. Officers were three to a similar tent, and one trio took their fire in with them, which must have been quite cosy, but the snag was - they never woke up next morning; very foolish idea to breathe carbon monoxide and sulphur dioxide, however cold the night.

One other item which has remained in my memory was the latrines which we dug. They were trenches, about six feet deep by ten or so feet long, and surmounted by a pole supported on two uprights. When the ground was frozen they were fairly safe, but in rainy weather, it needed some courage to position oneself with the pole half-way along the back of the thigh and only the adhesion of one's feet with the ground to prevent an involuntary backward somersault. It's better left to the reader's imagination, just what the dire possibilities might be to that situation.

It was January 1940 before our accommodation improved and we were installed in a row of Nissen huts on another and less cider-flavoured site, with facilities of a more modern standard, but not before quite a number of us went down with some kind of influenza.

Shortly after moving into these tents, we were allowed out of camp to explore the potential of the local settlement, Bougonnais. Food, naturally, was our first objective, and three of us found a typical cafe where we asked for ham and eggs in our best schoolboy French - and got, jambon et oeufs. The eggs were nicely fried as we expected but the jambon was thinly sliced cold boiled ham, and not at all to our taste. Nonetheless, it was scoffed with reasonable dispatch, and well washed down with bottles of the local wine. Too well washed perhaps, we up-graded our intake to champagne, which at 35 francs per bottle we could well afford - with francs at 180 to the £ - despite my rate of pay at 4s-6d per day. Not since that evening and its following two days have I cared much for that much vaunted bubbly wine: excess does often teach future caution in many directions.

After our inundation in the black dust of the hangar on arrival and our mud bath in erecting tents and digging trenches etc., among inches' deep of rotting apples, we were all ready for a bath, and were told that in Nantes there were public baths. A big city, Nantes, the sixth largest in France at that time, and sure enough, when three of us travelled the ten or so miles to find a public baths, we did. At first acquaintance, it appeared normal; a kiosk kind of office where we stated our wants, paid up and received towels and soap. We then waited until a bathroom was available, which was not long, and then two of us were shown into a bathroom with TWO baths in it and an attendant female running the water, etc. Well, we didn't mind bathing together in the same room (we lived together all the time), but we had some difficulty in persuading the attendant lady that we were quite capable of scrubbing our own backs, and thank you very much! The third one of our trio was not so successful in bathing alone, but he was probably much cleaner from the experience. On subsequent visits to this Bains Publiques, we were less shy; inhibitions are made to be shed.

It was during our attempts to find these baths that I received quite a blow to my amour-propre. Using my well-known common sense, I was asking a taxi-driver for directions to a public baths, in what I thought was reasonable French, when he interrupted me, "If you speak in English, I shall understand you much betters." I've heard this remark in other contexts; it must be the ultimate 'put-down'.

However, only a short distance from the baths we entered a restaurant, and here I did manage to hold my own; food even in my young days was fairly high on my list of interests. In this Hôtel Santeille, the three of us, Paddy O'Hanovrac, Wally Wareham and myself, enjoyed a meal fit for the kings we felt ourselves to be after scrubbing clean from the filth of the last couple of weeks.

Paddy and I were to use this restaurant almost exclusively whenever we had the luck to be in Nantes. Incidentally, Paddy came from Cork, and his name for RAF purposes was an anglicised one - which I forget - and in all likelihood I've not spelled his Gaelic name correctly.

For most of the latter end of 1939 we seemed to be performing repeats of our tasks at Henlow, that is, the building up of a large aircraft repair depot from scratch. Somebody, most likely the Royal Engineers, erected in what seemed to us no time at all, a hanger. This was close to the road from the village of Bougonnais to a small town about twenty miles away called Pornic.

Between this new Bellman hangar of ours and the first large hangar/workshop of the S.N.C.A.O., a squadron of the French Air Force were operating in conditions nearly as primitive as our own. Even their senior N.C.O.'s, who were at least in wooden huts, were sleeping on straw mattresses on the floors of those huts. I never saw how their lower ranks were accommodated. Even their aircraft were a bit historical; they were Breguet biplanes engaged in anti-submarine duties in the Bay of Biscay, and to carry out their duties they carried just one big fat bomb slung between the wheels of their undercarriages. This squadron attacked and sank a U-Boat during the time we were at Bougonnais, so they must have been able to fly at least as fast as a U-Boat sailed.

But more of our Allies later; our own new Bellman hangar was so quickly erected because it consisted mainly of a series of roughly twelve-inch square steel trellis work columns along the sides and rear, and across the roof-span. Some of the spaces between the uprights were filled with corrugated steel sheeting, and the doors, which faced onto the aerodrome, were just large canvas curtains.

In June of 1940 it was to take the Army even less time than the building of the structure to reduce it to ground level - by the judicious application of charges at the feet of the columns.

Alongside this hangar, we had been supplied with a mobile trailer machine-shop, containing a centre lathe, a small miller and a power-drill. The power to operate these machines and for our lighting in the hangar was to be supplied by another trailer equipped with a pair of Meadows 4 cyl, petrol engines driving a pair of AC generators, and a large switchboard.

Our personal toolkits were the standard issue dating in concept to about 1918, and contained some items rather primitive in design and manufacture. Others, like piano-wire cutters, were marvels of engineering ingenuity; it was a pity that we had no piano wire to cut for even in 1939 aircraft bracing wire had become streamlined in section (scrap 'wires' were often made into paper-knives by spare-time hobbyists).

There were also four-inch steel squares which I must admit were sometimes useful, and flat-nosed pliers which were practically useless - angled cutters would have been of far greater use for the oft-repeated job of removing split-pins, etc., without also removing skin from the knuckles.

There were a number of large flat packing cases which we were told contained our work-benches, other cases contained bench vices and specialist tools. When we opened these cases we found them to contain, not wooden benches, but large, six feet by three feet cast-iron surface tables of the kind which one would expect to find only one of in the tool-making shop or inspection department of a fairly large factory.

If we were going to do any work at all we were going to need benches, so we proceeded to drill holes in these tables to fit the vices, after we had manhandled them to suitable sites on the floor of the hanger. Those very accurately machined tables served quite well as benches, but just what Gerry made of such profligacy when they took over in '40 would be very interesting to hear.

Perhaps their amazement would have been balanced by the sight of the pile of scrapped airframes which grew alongside the hangar during our occupancy: for very soon after our arrival, engines and damaged airframes began to arrive in increasing numbers. Most of our work now consisted - as it had at Henlow - of dismantling these engines to form material for reassembly later; and most of the engines were Merlin II MS from Fairey Battles and Armstrong-Sidderley Tigers from Whitleys - the airframes were just junked into that large pile. Although we knew that Blenheims were also suffering losses, I don't remember seeing any Mercury engines turn up at Bougonnais; perhaps they went elsewhere, or were not recovered.

Life in France soon became as normal to us as peace-time home service; we even had church parades of a sort. Regular visits to Nantes for a change of diet, etc., and after our installation in Nissen huts after Christmas we, and by we I don't mean the whole unit, found a small farm nearby where the lady of the house would supply eggs and chips just like a NAAFI canteen - with the difference that we could accompany the dish with jugs of the local vino.

I have distinctive memories of sitting in the sun outside this old farmhouse playing a game we called 'Tippet', between teams either side of a trestle table loaded with glasses and jugs, until one by one the contestants subsided under the table. Most reprehensible!

Another farm which I visited from time to time was about half a mile away on the far side of a wood of coppiced brushwood. I was told by a local that this wood was cultivated for the source materials of basket-making, but its memories for me are of numerous nightingales belting away to each other on nights when I was doing guard duties along the road which bordered it. And there was the day when, taking my laundry along a glade through the wood, I heard what I thought was an aircraft, but which turned out to be an enormous hornet, about two inches long, which steamed along across my path whilst I stood paralysed.

The Frenchwoman who washed my shirts etc., lived in a one-roomed 'house' which was a part of the environs of a farm; a farm which obviously had a vineyard, because just outside her domicile was a circular, stone and concrete construction. This consisted of a wall about twenty-five feet in diameter enclosing a flat area, the centre of which held a pivot post around which a stone roller was operated to crush the grapes which were piled into the circular area. The juices expressed ran out through openings at the base of the wall.

Primitive as that may have been, it was quite advanced in comparison with the home of my laundress. This one single-storey room had one door, and one window about five feet square. The fire she cooked on and heated her dwelling by had no chimney, but the smoke was allowed to leave by way of a hole in the roof. She had a double bed and a small cot for herself and her two children and, presumably, also for her husband before his conscription into the French Army; the only other furniture I ever saw was a smallish table and a couple of chairs. Add this to the fact that the floor was of beaten earth, and it was truly remarkable how she managed to wash my clothing at all, never mind how she made such a good job of it!

This facet of the lives of ordinary French peasants, which showed from time to time that winter, made considerable excuse for the nation's lack of heart and enthusiasm to fight for a continuation of such conditions. Just how their Government expected any other reaction from their poilus than resentment and sheer indifference, when they took them from their families, paid them in chicken-feed and failed to provide any form of family allowances which I could ascertain, I don't know. We did much better than that, but even our efforts fell far short of those of the Canadian Government's.

Another illustration of the straits in which wives were left by this *soi~disant* civilised French government occurred on Christmas Eve.

Paddy and I went into Nantes for the usual bath and a good dinner: I kept the bill from that meal for a long time - at the end of the reckoning was a long column of a dozen or so items, Cognac 14 francs. We must have been well away when we left the restaurant, and we took with us a brown-paper carrier bag with a further bottle of brandy, several of wine and a syphon of soda water, for it was Christmas Day in the morning and there was no canteen at Château Bouguon.

We spent so long over that extended meal at the Santeuille that we missed the last transport back to those cosy little canvas homes of ours. Three choices were open to us, walk it, take a taxi - doubtful possibility this as local taxi-drivers had become rather disenchanted with British erks - or stay at a hotel in Nantes. The latter had the greater appeal, and a comrade had given us an address for such a chance need. We knew roughly where this place was, and bowled along there, carolling gently.

We met a British soldier en route, and chatted a little; when he heard the bottles clinking in our bag, he demanded a drink - which was not the best way to get one. Paddy said, "Shut your eyes and see what God'll send you." That squaddy must have been nearly as far gone as we were, for he did so, and Paddy gave him a generous squirt of soda-water, right down his throat that must have nearly drowned him.

Leaving the unfortunate brown job spluttering unhappily, we proceeded on our way to No. 28, Rue Scribe, where we knocked on the door, and were shown in. Inside we were introduced to several young ladies - and invited to choose one as a bed-mate!

Young we were, but the bed was the prime object of our desire on that cold night and in the advanced stage of our inebriation. Nevertheless, I recall that the bed-mate whom I chose insisted that I wash well before being allowed into her bed, and locked up our carrier bag in a cupboard to prevent further incursions into its contents, too. This girl could not have been more than twenty to twenty-two years old, and didn't really make much sense of my reaction to her enquiry, "Maintenant?" or of my answering that tomorrow was another day, but now was the time for sleep. It transpired next morning during conversation of the limited kind one could expect to have after only a couple of months or so in a foreign country, that she was married, with a young child, and that her husband was in the French Army on two-and-a-half francs a day, although he DID have a wine and cigarette issue. There, thought Paddy and I, would be another citizen who would perhaps be glad that war was over for them when the balloon went up in 1940.

But this account was intended to be more amusing than poignant, so the tale of the extended church parade might be interposed here. Church parades in the RAF and Navy are based on the Anglican Church of England, so before any actual religious activity takes place, Roman Catholics, Jews, and any other denominations are instructed to 'fall out'; fall out of the ranks, that is, not fall out with their comrades. Here in France we had no Jews with us, and other denoms kept very quiet; only our few RC's felt the need for a little communion with God. Paddy, being one of those wild Gaels, was one of them. On one never-to-be-forgotten Sunday, a pick-up truck was laid on to take Paddy and one other - a Londoner, whose name I fear I forget - to a RC service at a church in a village about five miles away, called Pont St. Martin. As I was without a duty, I decided to go along with them for the ride and whatever could be arranged for after the service. The driver of the pick-up dropped us in St. Martin, and the two lads toddled dutifully into church, the driver went off with the remark that we should easily be able to find our own way back; and I wandered around the village.

There was a small stream running through - and under the Pont - which I followed a little way, until I spied a small row-boat, drawn up to the bank. "That would be a nice idea," I thought. "We'll go for a row to work up a thirst." It was easy to find the owner of the boat, it was such a small place, and he was willing to hire it to us for very little, and provide the oars. These oars were the shortest ones I'd ever seen, and we were to find out just why they needed to be so curtailed.

Meeting Paddy and his co-worshipper after the service, they fell in with the idea willingly, and we set off downstream with one to steer with the rudder, and one to row. Instead of getting wider, as one could expect downstream, the stream seemed to narrow, and solid land retreated behind thicker and thicker growths of quite high reeds. Hence the short oars: anything longer than six feet would have fouled the reed-beds. Nevertheless, we continued, and eventually, the stream opened right out and we found ourselves on a lake. From our height just above water-level, we could just see the other side of the lake and made out what looked like a beach with boats drawn up onto it. "Let's go and investigate over there, it looks bigger than St. Martin." We did just that, managing to take it in turns to row without any great upset although the boat did rock a little during take-over. On arrival at the far side, it was found that the beach was that gooey mud that often occurs in the bottom of tidal harbours, so we prospected a bit along the coast where we found a sort of private creek with a nice jetty. Here we disembarked and strolled through someone's garden and into the village street, where we soon identified and entered the local café. To our surprise, the place was well occupied with young folk, and they were congregated in a large room with, of all things, a juke-box. This gadget was playing those sort of tunes which Frenchmen always play on accordions, and we didn't hesitate to join in the dancing, in-between assuaging the thirst engendered by the long row. Being naturally, more flush with francs than this group of youngsters (even younger than we were), it fell to us to feed the machine, which we did willingly and everyone had a great time. But lunch was calling our new friends, and we were also in need of a bite. Two of these lads and their sister took it upon themselves to invite us three erks to join them for déjeuner, and we accepted. Strange as it seems the parents actually welcomed us and we sat down at the table. Even stranger, to me at least, was the dish. There were eight of us, three youngsters, their parents and three starving erks. On the table was a jug of water, a couple of bottles of wine, several jars of different jams - which Madame called 'conserves' - and the plates etc. When Madame brought lunch from the kitchen, I was amazed - it was the largest omelette I'd ever seen, and it was more than adequate for all of us there, together with that lovely crisp baked French bread.

The time soon came when we had to make our way back across that lake, a thought which had been left in limbo whilst enjoying ourselves so much. We started off quite well, despite the load of wine we carried and the loss of energy from all the dancing before lunch. It was at about the half-way mark that we began to have qualms: the whole horizon before us of the coast we were headed for looked just like a reed-bed - where the hell was our river-mouth? This was not our only trouble, there was more. The effort of rowing was such that we took off our tunics very soon, but as the day began to close, the air cooled down and so did the non-rowers. It was during one of the change-overs of position that Paddy - or the cockney, I forget which - fell over the side with tunic half-on, fairly hilarious to us other dry-clad sailors, as we dragged our unfortunate fellow crewman aboard, with infinite care not to join him in the pawney. How that was actually safely accomplished remains a real mystery; the boat took upon itself some quite unusual attitudes in the process. Not only were we getting a little cold now, but were also a bit damp, and it was going to take us a lot longer to find the entrance to our river than it had taken us to cross the lake during the morning. We did, though, if after one or two false starts among the reeds, find the mouth of the stream and arrived at Pont St. Martin around midnight. It only remained then for we weary travellers to navigate about five miles of country roads back to Bougonnais; with many wrong turns, we managed to arrive not long after the sun rose.

Soon after Christmas we moved into the new Nissen huts, just in time, as it happened, for me to spend three days in bed on a diet of tea, by means of the good offices of Paddy, and aspirins and Dover's Powders from an overcrowded sick-quarters to drive out a dose of the current influenza. After this was cleared up and before our little sailing adventure across the Lac de Grande Lieu my turn for a spot of leave came up - leave for which we were given the choice of ten days in Paris, Marseilles or Blighty. Very imaginatively, I chose to risk the U-boats in the Channel and give the old folks a glimpse of a war hero! Pity I didn't realise that some of that ten days would be spent in travel, but one can't think of everything.

At the close of the Spanish Civil War, Franco's forces drove a large remnant of the defeated red Government forces into Catalonia up against the French borders in the Eastern Pyrenees. For a long time they were not allowed to cross into France but as eventually it became obvious that if they remained trapped there, they would be for the high jump; they were permitted to cross and were placed in a refugee camp somewhere near to Bougonnais. I never found out where this camp was, but often saw gangs of them being marched to some sort of work, under the control of the French National Guard. These gentlemen walked alongside the refugees in their smart black uniforms, which included patent-leather high boots, belt, holster and kepi, and were wielding actual whips to supplement their automatic pistols. A sorry lot, the Spaniards looked.

The S.N.C.A.O. factory was engaged in the assembly of a single-seater fighter aircraft, the Morane Saulnier 405 and 406: this kite had Hispano-Suiza 20 mm cannon nestling between the cylinder blocks of its V-12 engine which fired through the prop boss. The six or so of these A/C produced per day were ground tested on the tarmac apron in front of their hangar and the cannon also were tested - in the tail on the ground position!! Nobody I spoke to ever found out just where those shells were landing, but there was a strong rumour that most of them came to earth very close to the camp where the Spanish refugees were retained.

There were bombers also assembled at Bougonnais but rather less than one a day as I recall. These were the Loiré 45, which had twin contra-rotating radial engines. It also had treaded tyres on the undercarriage with brushes fitted to clean the tread and avoid grit etc., from flying up into the props. Most aircraft at that date had smooth tyres, but nowadays treaded ones are commonplace.

As 1940 rolled on into early spring, we still seemed to be acting as some kind of scrap merchants for the RAF contingent of the B.E.F.: the most constructive job which I remember doing was the refuelling of visiting aircraft. On one occasion I was tending the Meadows in the generator trailer when called to a fill-up task, and, jumping down from the trailer onto a plank laid on the surrounding mud, sprained an ankle badly as the plank tilted and ended up in dock.

The hospital was at La Baule, where the casino of all places had been taken over as a sick-bay. Perhaps our allies had little need for further games of chance after gambling that the Maginot Line would prevent an invasion of France when it could just be walked around at either end! However, discounting the pain, that week at La Baule was a pleasant interlude. Not that life was unpleasant by now; the weather was rapidly improving and our domestic condition was also showing signs of almost peace-time normality. We even had a French news vendor to supply copies of the Continental Daily Mail, who also taught me how to swear in the local patois.

There were weekly issues of free cigarettes, frequent parcels of 'comforts'; pullovers, knitted gloves, and sometimes very welcome socks - most of us had at least one balaclava helmet by June. Gerry no doubt found these very useful as their heads cooled in Russia after '41.

Some idea of the change in the weather from our tented period in the orchard - when the temperature was often in the minus 30°s C - when I mention that in May we were buying fresh strawberries - and at 7 francs per kilogram, we bought plenty.

Our financial situation vis-à-vis our grossly underpaid allies of the neighbouring Breguet squadron must have been a direct comparison with OUR attitude to the free-spending - and thus general price-raising - of those other allies who came in to help US when they thought that perhaps their investments in aid might not be paid for if we lost.

Thinking of money, reminds me of those tiny spiders which we call money spiders, and of one lovely sunny day of early summer when the air became full of a kind of misty veil, being carried on a light breeze from a wood beyond the village, and away, over the 'drome. It was almost impossible to avoid being covered by some of this, and it proved to be the self-produced aerial mode of transport of countless thousands of tiny Gossamer spiders.

The wood where they had originated before their mass emigration was used, I was told, for the cultivation of those large snails which the French find so delicious. I must say, I never plucked up sufficient courage to try them, and yet never missed the chance of starting a meal, when in Nantes, with half a dozen Portuguais Vertes, which look even less appetising as their pale green bodies throb gently on the shell.

An interesting and almost fairy-tale-like episode occurred when a De Haviland Dominie made a false landing a few miles away and a small party of us were sent out to mount guard on the wreck until it could be salvaged. Only a few days before, I had been assisting in the refuelling of this D.H. 89, using those paper-thin four gallon tins in which both DTD 224 and DTD 230 aviation spirit were transported - the tins were often half-empty from leaks, but did come in handy for building air-raid shelters, etc., when filled with sand.

A corporal, Wally Wareham, myself and four others went off with a few days' rations, some directions, and high hopes of finding the Dominie, which, strangely enough, we did at almost the first attempt.

There was a large pair of ornamental gates opening from what would be in England, a second class country lane, but beyond the gates was a straight gravel drive down the centre of a stretch of grass about a hundred yards wide between two rows of trees. At the end of the drive, some three hundred yards away, was a great house with a gravelled area in front of the main entrance. Running across the avenue in front of this area, an ornamental stream flowed and the drive crossed this by means of a fairly narrow bridge with a low parapet. For whatever reason, the Dominie pilot had seen the long drive and had put his kite down very nicely, to the point when he was still rolling as he reached the bridge - which was narrower than his undercart. When we found it, it had the port wheel on the bridge and the starboard wheel in the brook, with the starboard wing looking rather crumpled, also in the water.

Well, we had a three-tonner with canvas top as home, plenty of food, and good weather. We also had rifles for the guard duty, but I couldn't resist removing the Verey pistol from its rack in the DH, and putting a couple of signal cartridges in my pocket. Wally and I then wandered off to reconnoitre the countryside; and the first objective was the château, which turned out to belong to the Prefect of Police of Nantes. They pay their police well in this country, we thought; and no doubt we were right - in this case.

Wandering around the rear areas, we found enough other buildings for a small village, including a row of workers' cottages with a large pond in front of them. By this time there were several of the château staff around and there was much entente cordiale going on in a mixture of French and arm-waving. One of our new-found friends spotted the two-inch bore of the Verey pistol which was stuck in my tunic belt like a Chicago gangster's gat and was giving it, as his considered opinion, that if these Anglais had arms like that, the Boche didn't stand a chance. Not to let the side down, I decided to give a demo, and loaded with a double red cartridge. There were ducks paddling around on that pond and it struck me that one would add interest to our immediate diet, so I drew a bead on one and fired the cannon. Of course I missed. There was a gasp from the audience, a startled quack from the duck, and a bit of a sizzle as the flare hit the water. Unfortunately, it didn't sink, but played ducks and drakes across the pond to end up in a hedge on the far side - and set it on fire! Not a very auspicious beginning to our sojourn.

Nevertheless, we were obviously forgiven - or needed to be treated with respect and deference - because one of those local gentlemen showed us around the buildings, which included the wine store. This we considered really vast, a large building in which there were four rows of barrels with what must have been a dozen barrels per row - and what barrels! Eight feet high, if an inch, and the same in diameter.

Wally and I were given a glass apiece and told to sample any which had a tap connected. For the rest of our stay at that château it was not often we were seen elsewhere than in that store, and we were all quite sorry to greet the crew who came to relieve us; well, who wouldn't be?

CHAPTER 13
St. Nazaire and Floristan

The four months of semi-hardship under canvas passed almost unremarked into the next four months of much better conditions from February to May, in which we not only made progress towards becoming a viable repair depot, but also found the time and energy to enjoy ourselves. This, of course, was the period of what became known as the 'Phoney War'. Phoney it may have been to sensation-hungry news hawks anxious only to file their quota of reports at so much per word, but sailors on the high seas had known differently from that September Sunday morning of '39; and the troops in Scandinavia found that life was no ski-ing holiday. Even had they been holidaying, the two weeks spent in Norway would hardly have been time enough to learn how to order a beer before they, or what was left of them, were evacuated.

We had no sooner digested the grievous results of the northern 'campaign' than news kept arriving of action in the east, OUR east. When on leave in January, I had stressed to my folks in the English midlands that at Nantes I was actually further away from any part of Germany than they were: it was beginning to look as if that was not going to be the case for very much longer.

Still with what may be called the holiday spirit, Paddy and I took a local diesel bus to Pornic on one weekend in May. This was - probably still is - a small fishing harbour and village with a rocky coast very similar to many places on our Cornish coast.

By this time we were often seeing Belgian and some French refugees passing the aerodrome, usually with many of their possessions piled into their cars and lorries. They were easily identified as refugee vehicles by the mattresses carried on top as a fancied protection from strafing aircraft. One vehicle which we saw parked near the harbour at Pornic was an articulated Mercedes pantechnicon which had been converted into a two-storey motor-caravan.

One sometimes wonders just what is the right action to take when one's country is invaded. Does one stay and make life difficult for the enemy - and oneself - or skedaddle as quick as possible and leave as little behind as possible?

The people of Holland, Luxembourg and Belgium had this decision to make and most of them decided to stay, with varying thoughts on future action. To stop resistance to what was an irresistible force and thus to prevent the destruction to their country which might have been the alternative, seems quite sensible to me, but must have taken some considerable courage. The refugees on the other hand were something of a nuisance to the fighting forces who were hampered by finding roads blocked by civilian vehicles.

But be that as it may, many of the refugees we now saw were our own troops, often ground staff who having no longer any kites to service felt little would be gained by staying around. There was a second BEF sent over to France after the Dunkirk evacuation but our enemy was moving too quickly for them to have much effect, and the panzers rolled on.

Much of this second BEF was Blighty-bound via Cherbourg, and harbours in north and western Brittany like St. Mâlo and St. Nazaire: and after Paris was occupied on June 14th, it was our turn to pack up our troubles in the old kitbag - and march!

But first we had to see that anything left would give no comfort to Gerry. There was a fair amount of aviation spirit in those thin 4 gal tins, which we had some fun in puncturing with a pickaxe and when sufficient was flowing, in burning - if burning is the word for the WHOOSH it made. What didn't give any pleasure in burning was a couple of Magister aircraft, one of which had only two hours' of flying life. This one I was sadly tempted to essay an attempt at flying home, but some wiser friend, in telling me that the Maggie had a tendency to corkscrew on take off because of reaction to propeller rotation, sufficiently quenched my enthusiasm. So two sweet little aeroplanes went up in smoke. It was with some regret that I didn't see the hangar flattened, there were no pleasant memories of tasks performed therein.

And now it was our turn to leave Bougonnais; most had departed, and we had to commandeer a White truck from the French to catch up with them. There was an aerodrome near St. Nazaire which was in process of being built as a terminus for the trans-Atlantic route. There were a couple of new hangars - these, unlike the one at Bougonnais, had a smooth concrete floor - and the 'drome was criss-crossed with drainage ditches; and it was here we were told to wait for further movement orders. On this 17th day of June the sun was very pleasant as we lay about on the grass or in the hangars until some obviously hostile aeroplanes appeared, but seemed not to be interested and passed on; but shortly we were made aware that they'd found something to interest them. It was that afternoon that the liner, Lancastria was bombed and sunk in St. Nazaire harbour, when over 3000 of the 5800 troops aboard her were lost. Little was known in Blighty about this disastrous event, it transpired that those who did know thought it better not to discourage the populace with such small setbacks: brave words from politicians were a much more nourishing diet for a country still suffering from their Dunkirk mêlée.

Having lain in some of those ditches on the airfield until we ached, it was a relief to be marched off. But before leaving there was some light refreshment to be had. A large NAAFI truck pulled onto the 'drome and someone with more than a modicum of common sense told them that there was no chance they'd be able to get that lot into any ship so they might as well dish its contents out to the troops right there. In that truck there was tinned fruit, chocolate, tobacco, in fact all those items which erks treated themselves to in the canteens and the NAAFI bod just stood in the back of his truck and flung stuff out to the milling troops. I only managed to obtain one tin of fruit, but collected several hundred Woodbines in 200's plus a few tins of Phillips pipe tobacco, to make room for which in my kitbag, I needed to dispose of some kit items.

I was not the only one to junk good kit: in peregrinations around the aerodrome I picked up a short Lee-Enfield Mk III* rifle which some bod had decided was too heavy to carry further and to make this bundook operational I looked around for ammo. There were a couple of squaddies dismantling a Vickers machine-gun nearby, as part of our scorched-earth policy, and I collected a mixed hundred or so rounds from the belt. There were tracer, armour-piercing, and Buckingham explosive rounds as well as ordinary ball in that belt, and there was enough ammo in my haversack to sink a life-raft if we'd sunk on the way home.

It must have been several miles from that half-finished aerodrome to the docks at St. Nazaire, and at one point in our march we were deflected into a field of mowing grass in order to allow an artillery unit to pass. They were complete with guns, towing trucks and limbers, etc. A fat chance they would have of getting that lot away, we thought, after seeing the episode of the NAAFI truck, and this proved to be the case, for the whole caboodle was dumped into the harbour. But we were not consulted for our opinion, and were just left to wait for them to pass and to doze away the afternoon in the sun.

It was in that field that I saw grasshoppers which were a bright green and about four inches long in the body; there were hundreds of them zizzing away and jumping all over us.

Eventually we arrived at St. Nazaire dockyards, and there at the wall was a civvy freighter, the Floristan, in which we would, if lucky, be sailing home. At this juncture, there was a bit of a kerfuffle, as some French policemen were making an attempt to prevent the embarkation of our leg-weary party on this boat. Suddenly, they seemed to disappear, and there were splashing sounds. It was never quite clear whether they thought we were to be prevented from deserting them in their hour of desperate need, or were perhaps making some attempt to curry favour with our joint enemy - who by this time were just a matter of a few thousand yards behind us.

As it was getting dusk and the tide in the Loire was on the ebb, we were hustled aboard in fairly quick time.

Among our numbers, which we later learned was over 3000, were many who had been rescued from the Lancastria, and many others who had been fighting the same kind of rearguard action which had taken place to enable Operation Dynamo to be so successful a month before. Some of these others had retained their weapons and they were to prove useful. On that moonlit first night, as we moved slowly down the Loire Estuary, we had a visit from a lone Junkers 88, who thought he could emulate his Luftwaffe comrade and bag a nice soft target, but the 'shot and shell' which was thrown at him as he was inadvised enough to pass across the face of the moon was effective enough, for he took a steep dive into the water with plain signs that SOME form of fire extinguisher was required. The ship's armament - a lone Lewis on the bridge - was credited with the victory. But there were at least two Bren guns resting on the starboard rail, and dozens of rifles banging away - one of our RAF sergeants was pumping .45 from his Webley and Scott pocket cannon. I also watched a pair of squaddies operating a Boyes anti-tank rifle as a team, one firing from the shoulder with his mate supporting him from behind by standing at forty-five degrees to him so that the recoil wouldn't put him flat on his back - not that there was really room for anyone to fall over on that crowded deck.

Floristan had a centre section which contained the bridge and the crew's quarters etc., with a raised poop deck aft and a raised foredeck forward, in between each raised deck and the bridge structure were the cargo holds. In this ship they were two-storeyed and it was my bad luck to be directed into the lower forward hold. Among the troops with me down there were a number of Indian Army Sikh cavalrymen, turbans, long tunics and breeches, and with large brass-handled swords hanging from their belts. As we'd had to climb down rope ladders to reach this haven of unrest about ten feet below sea-level, the thought occurred to me that should the worst come to the worst, I should stand less chance of drowning than of getting my head chopped off in the rush for the ladder!

However, we moved away from the quay and reversed down river on the ebb tide, an unfortunate result of which hurried departure was that we fouled something on the bottom, and caused - I was told later - a loosening of seven of the ship's bottom plates. This so upset the captain that he decided that we must steam very slowly in order to retain what was left of our hull in one piece, a sentiment which it seems did not appeal overmuch to the captain of the only destroyer escort remaining for he decided that he had a war to fight elsewhere and good luck chaps.

But this I learned next day after a night stewing in the hold. There was a hail from the patch of light which we could see filtering down through the upper hold.

"Anybody down there knows anything about kites?"

It was the second officer of the ship. "I do," I shouted quick as a flash and was echoed by a fellow internee. This voice came from Ike Poole, who was an airframe fitter.

"Well, get yourselves here quick! I need you," came from the civvy sailor.

Need I say that we both needed no second instruction and were up that ladder like a pair of scalded monkeys. Joining our saviour, he took us up onto the foredeck where he opened a locker and said, "There it is. Let's have it out here." It was a collection of bamboo poles and canvas sheets together with great coil of rope and, under the watchful eye of the matelot we sorted it out and found it to be a giant box-kite - it must have been twenty feet by about five feet square when we finally assembled it, not easy on that small deck with a breeze running at about five to six knots. We did it though, and with one end of the rope fixed to the kite and the other passed around a windlass affair up forward. I was feeding the rope out while Ike and the second officer lifted that crazy toy up until the wind caught it and away it went, by the time Ike joined me on the rope, my fingers and palms were a bit the worse for wear. I've made kites as a lad, but never one which flew as perfectly as that one did, it sailed away as steady as a rock, about 2-300 feet above and to starboard of us, and all we had left to do was sit up there and watch it from the comfort of a large coil of mooring hawser. There was more than a few moments of unrest in the soul when we were made aware of the presence on the horizon of a FW Condor which was obviously keeping an eye on us for one of his submarine mates, but perhaps his radio had a flat battery or he thought our kite was a Spitfire, because no sub turned up.

After a whole day up there with Ike, we began to feel hungry and we could see a queue forming along the starboard side of the ship with bods coming away with mugs of something. We'd had nothing since the feast of fruit on the 'drome at St. Nazaire, so decided to take turns in the queue. I went first and managed to collect a tin of bully and a mug of tea but when I tried to get back to the kite flying area, I was assailed by army types who declared that deck was out of bounds! One place I was NOT going back to was that lower hold, and wandered slowly aft. Climbing up the ladder to the poop deck, I saw that there was a small boat in its davits up there, with several airmen sitting in it. Without further ado, I stepped over the low rail and into this boat; not until we reached old Blighty's shore did I leave it. The consequence of salt spray was the peeling-off of my facial skin, leaving a very weatherbeaten look to it. This old-salt appearance gave ample scope for a great line-shoot whilst on leave, about having spent three days in an open boat without - of course - my mentioning that the boat had still been hanging in its davits!

I suppose that we were only at sea for a matter of four days all told, which was just as well considering that the tin of bully-beef I'd collected was my total subsistence until docking at Falmouth. The damage to Floristan was such that she had to put into Falmouth instead of proceeding to Southampton where the remainder of the convoy were scheduled for; a convoy which we had been fated not to join - or even see!

When those quarter million or so of troops which were rescued from the beaches of Dunkirk returned to Blighty, the reception they received was that of returning heroes. They had, it soon became known, put up a magnificent rearguard action and deserved their welcome, which was no doubt tinged with sympathy, for retreating is not really the most potent of ego-boosters. A similar kudos was not, so far as most of us were concerned, really applicable, but our treatment on arrival in England showed that we were being classed with those Operation Dynamo types. On our disembarkation at Falmouth, we were made to feel quite important by being met by young recruits from RAF Locking, who insisted on carrying our kits for us to the trucks awaiting us. And when at Locking, they gave up their beds for us and themselves slept on the barrack-room floor.

Any euphoria this engendered was quickly dispelled next morning, when a roll-call was held on the barrack square. As the name of each unit or squadron was called, the personnel of that unit were to step out and line up together. When one squadron's number was called, only a single man stepped out - his unit had been in the Lancastria and he was the sole survivor.

At Locking we were given a pay parade, leave passes, and rail-warrants to our home towns, with instructions to await further instructions at home. So off I went via London, taking with me the salvaged rifle, ammunition, the not-to-be-forgotten kitbag full of tobacco products; all of which I had somewhat miraculously managed to recover from the ship's hold at Falmouth.

CHAPTER 14
Norfolk and an Active Squadron

Staying overnight at the Union Jack Club en route home and relishing somewhat the feeling of being the darlings of Fate whom nothing could assail, three of us went out to investigate war-time London's night-life. There did not seem to be much of that, but wandering up Regent Street, we stopped in the entrance of a cinema which was showing Disney's Pinnochio, and while we were looking at stills, the commissionaire came up behind us and said, "Come on in, lads, there's plenty of room in the stalls and it's just starting." We must have looked a poor lot - scruffy, no gas-masks, and I wasn't even wearing a cap, for a tin-hat had been more suitable for the last few days - but this was a welcome change from being barred from my favourite pub in Hitchen just before leaving for France.

There was no exclusion from the pubs in my home town, and I made the most of that leave. During it I bought a secondhand motor cycle - a Triumph model X 250 cc two-stroke - for £10: an optimistic purchase perhaps, but it was to prove useful later, when operating on satellite landing grounds in East Anglia.

Eventually, a letter arrived with instructions to report to No. 18 Squadron at RAF West Raynham in Norfolk by the 6th of July, and enclosing a railway-warrant. "Norfolk," I thought, "I'll need the bike there. No RAF station is nearer than five miles from the nearest pub." And so it was to prove.

Whilst at Bougonnais, in fact almost as soon as my 'props' were through, I had volunteered for aircrew, and had passed the medical. There was obviously more than a little confusion with paperwork as with all other aspects of the RAF administration during our rather rapid departure from the land of frogs, because there was never any follow-up from that selection and medical.

The Squadron I joined were equipped with long-nosed Blenheim IV's, and in the first few weeks after my arrival they were operating against shipping in the North Sea, with what struck me as disastrous losses of men and machines. For some months there hung over my mind a feeling of impending doom, for it was beginning to look as if there was going to be little future in flying - a short life and a gay one perhaps - but as the months went on with no call for me, I stopped worrying and settled down to keeping those who DID fly as well served as possible.

Almost before I had settled down on my new Station, life began to fill with exciting happenings: excitement not always of the kind which comes first to mind.

Being a part of a real operational squadron was new to me if one ignores that ten days or so spent with 43 Squadron at Tangmere almost a year ago and it gave me a feeling of being more a member of the RAF than previous postings which had been always to FTS's and Repair Depots. Not to decry such jobs, but squadron life always had seemed to me to be more desirable - perhaps on the principle of the grass being greener, etc...

West Raynham was - still is - situated not more than fifteen miles from the coast, and it was early discovered that any warning it received of impending enemy air activity was of very short duration. It may have been the thought of possible petrol shortages in any war making it useful not to waste it in flying over home territory during attack missions. The net result had, however, been recognised and the newish barrack blocks there were models of modernity, with built-in air-raid shelters, so that the occupants needed not to expose themselves to the elements if off duty during visits by the Luftwaffe. There were other shelters dotted around the camp of the same type, more or less as those built for schoolchildren: a large half-round steel corrugated sheeting job, well dug-in, with escape ladder and hatch at one end and brick steps at the other end; the whole covered with from two to three feet of earth, and safe from anything but a direct hit. There were also quite good trenches between the two large hangars and the perimeter track running across in front. These hangars were of the same type which was being built at Thornaby in 1937, with offices and stores attached along the side nearest to the 'drome.

I had not been at Raynham more than four days when we had a dawn raid by some intruding Gerry, who lobbed a bomb or three - about 25 kilogram ones, but they make quite a bang - into the No. 1 hangar, and destroyed an Anson or two plus a Gladiator. Venturing to poke my inquisitive nose around the two feet or so gap between the hangar doors, it struck me as a remarkable testimonial to the wooden beam construction of the Anson main spar that the one nearest to the doors was blackened and smouldering, but the engines were on the deck beneath in a nearly molten state. I never examined the scene more closely, because at the moment I poked my silly head in, the oxygen bottle or the compressed-air reservoir of the Gauntlet exploded. Well, the Luftwaffe did have the habit of leaving delayed action crackers around!

Whether it was this raid or a later one I don't recall, but on one occasion a bomb was dropped very low on the airfield and skidded across the grass to enter the side building of No. 2 hangar. By bad luck it pierced the outer wall of the crew-room, which contained rows of steel lockers. These lockers were where the aircrews kept their parachutes, Irvin flying jackets, helmets, etc. The explosion of this single bomb inside that crew-room packed these lockers to either end of the room so tightly that our unhappy flyers found it very difficult to extract their gear from the resulting multi-sandwich of steel, silk and leather.

Much could be written of the official activities of 18 Squadron, and most of it has been, and can be found in the official histories; this is only the idiosyncratic reminiscences of one of its lesser members. The actively offensive (and to the enemy, offensively active) parts of the Squadron moved to a satellite 'drome at Great Massingham in September, but HQ Flight remained at Raynham, so it seemed that my fate was still to be one of the back-room boys as it were: one of the lucky ones too as it turned out, because they had a rather unpleasant time of it when Gerry visited them at Massingham in October.

But with the coast so near, we were also to receive further attentions. One lunchtime as I was going from the hangar to my billet, the siren sounded, an event which it was always wise to take seriously in eastern Norfolk.

There was one of those shelters described above nearby, just behind the sick-bay, so I, and several other bods stepped down gently. Not wanting to miss anything exciting which might ensue, two or three of us stood on the steps with our heads about level with the deck, and looked around. Suddenly we spotted an aircraft at about 500 feet and coming our way from westwards, over the Officers' Mess. Just at that moment he released a stick of bombs which were clearly visible - and also coming our way!

We'd seen enough of that aircraft for the moment and dived rapidly into the body of the shelter: there was the usual crump, crump, as the first of the stick exploded, and then the shelter IN

TOTO rocked first one way then the other and we thought - at least I did - that we'd had it this time. But we hadn't, when the coast seemed clear we crept from what was indeed a shelter, to see that the earth covering had been cleared away from both sides, leaving the tin case almost fully exposed for most of its length.

There was a tale around the camp afterwards that one of the stick had dropped on the barrack square - what better place? - and that an airman who was running across to shelter had been alongside the explosion. He was found in the bottom of the crater with no sign of injury, except that he was unconscious. Whether this was an apocryphal tale or not, I never found out, but there was certainly a nice big crater in the middle of the square.

What was not so doubtful, happened on the occasion of a short visit one evening by a marauding Dopple Acht, when one of the lads was caught in the open near the billet and avoided the effect of a short burst from the air-gunner by dodging around a handy tree near the barrack blocks. Not to be cheated of their bit of fun the 88 did a quick bank around the tree to give me laddo in the dorsal turret another try; glad to say with no more success than the first burst had, so called it a day and disappeared rapidly before local opposition made their stay permanent.

Although it is not my intention to list all those little occasions when the odd bomb stirred us up a bit, it must be recounted that on one early evening, a number of delayed-action bombs were scattered across the airfield among our dispersed aircraft.

Our Chiefy, Flt/Sgt Clampitt, being a concerned sort of chappie, looked around the 'drome and found some of these DA's too close to our Blenheims for his peace of mind - after all, HE was in charge of repairs; so he roused out a couple or so of us to help shift those kites in immediate danger. With him driving the towing tractor, and two of us to lift the tail wheel into its little box on the tail-trolley and hitch up the towlines, we spent a hair-raising half hour or so moving kites around the field in the dark until Chiefy was happy - well, as happy as possible.

It was difficult, next morning, to decide whether laughing or crying would be most appropriate - at least one of those we had so laboriously shifted was now placed exactly above an ugly great fat DA.

Because of all this excitement, and because Raynham was so easily found and identified, the flights were mostly on the move to various satellites, but the hangars at least offered a decent place to work on aircraft, and the billets a great advance on camping out in some old farm building.

About this time I managed to grab a weekend leave pass, and when I returned I brought back my old Triumph 2-stroke; at least it brought me. Interesting, that night ride from Wolves to Raynham; at the average speed of which the little Triumph was capable - about 25 mph I suppose.

In Britain ALL signposts had been eliminated to avoid offering directional aid to possible enemy parachutists, we were told but the roads remained, and in those unenlightened days they actually led from one town or village to another, and often had some locally recognisable feature as a help. Now, on the contrary, they avoid built-up areas, all look alike, and the traveller is very lucky if they even follow the general direction in which he desires to go. Try to follow a general compass course across England and one could end up just anywhere nowadays.

On that night in 1940, I had no trouble-at all in finding my route, until just before Peterborough, when I was flagged down by a hitch-hiking squaddy. As we rode on I asked him to show me the best exit from Peterborough for my next objective, Downham Market. In the city centre he directed me very well and we proceeded happily for several miles until he indicated that he was near his own destination. After dropping him I carried on as instructed - until I noted that due north was NOT my true route. Some distance past P'borough there is a length of absolutely straight road for about six miles and this should have been long reached, so I turned back to P'borough and started again from there. It was lucky for that army bod that I never met him again. That stretch of road had a sharp kink about half way along it which needed thinking about when lying along the tank with the throttle fully open, a left followed immediately by a right - tricky if one is being lulled into a doze by the loneliness of the road and the unaltering exhaust note.

It was not long after returning to Raynham, that I sold off the little bike, and plunged an extra couple of quid into buying a 350 cc Raleigh, a much more exciting - but far less reliable - mount. It was on this monster that I returned to Norfolk one summer night in 1941, without the vestige of a light because the dynamo was kaput and battery ditto. Not until I was on the Norwich ring-road, and halted to check that I was at my turn off for Horsham, was I challenged: a voice from the shadows said, "Where's your lights then, lad?" My answer was to drop the clutch and open the throttle very smartly, with quite excellent results.

Life continued for some time at what could be described as normal for a squadron in war-time Britain, there at Raynham; work on aircraft, sleeping time, playing at cards - usually games like Brag or Solo Whist - and trips to either the village of Raynham for a pint, or farther afield to Fakenham, where there was a very good Salvation Army unit which provided excellent eggs and chips. One of the most regrettable events of that period of the war was when that Sally-Ann was bombed; Gerry must have known that it was a source of high morale for the erks in that part of Norfolk.

There were, I recall, one or two visits to the station of ENSA concert parties, and these too helped to keep the lads happy, but by and large, we managed to cope fairly well. Christmas '41 saw us with actual BUCKETS of beer in the barrack-room; a situation which was unheard of in peace-time as can well be imagined.

Back in the summer of '40, I had had a little argument with Chiefy Clampitt on a technical matter. One of our Blenheims had suffered shrapnel damage to a push-rod on one engine, and it was given to me to replace it. These push-rods were low-carbon steel tubes with hardened steel inserts at top and bottom. Drawing a new rod from stores, I found that it was just the tube which had to be made exactly the correct length before fitting the hardened ball ends. It completely foxed me as to just how I was to measure the length of the complete rod without first fitting the ends. Unfortunately the manual for the Mercury VIII gave no hint that I could find as to how one removed the ball-ends in order to file the tube to such length that it would be correct when re-assembled: these ends were a tight press fit. My way was to measure TWO new tubes to fit the ends, fit them to the engine, check for length, then remove the ends from the first tube, file the second tube to correct length and fit the ends to the second. Presto, a new rod fitted, and of the correct length. Chiefy did not approve of using engine spares in such cavalier fashion however, and it so happened that only very shortly after that, my corporal's stripes came through - and Chiefy, in his wisdom, put a six months' delay on my promotion. This delay was brought forward a bit but nevertheless, the hiatus continued of course, through subsequent promotions. I must have paid in lost pay rises, much more then the cost of a push-rod tube, but the aircraft WAS made serviceable!

Sometime in the early spring of '41, 'B' Flight moved to a new satellite field at Oulton, near Aylesham. Here a few hedges had been grubbed out to give a large enough landing ground, and then their old sites had been simulated by painting them in with tar: something of a waste of effort really, as any airman worthy of the name can recognise an aerodrome when he sees one.

About the beginning of May '41, this Flight was detached to Portreath, a cliff-top aerodrome near St. Ives, with the object, the buzz went round, of livening up the crews of a couple of German Battle-wagons, the Scharnhorst and the Gneisenhau, usually known as Salmon and Gluckstein after the well known tobacconists.

A few of us from HQ Flight at Raynham were detailed to accompany the flight and we lifted down to Cornwall in a Bristol Bombay. This was, by modern standards, a smallish transport aircraft, where passengers provided their own seats with their kitbags.

As we climbed into the Bombay, there was a quite strong smell of aviation spirit from what turned out to be a small leak in the fuselage fuel tank. We were pretty aghast - at least, I was - to hear the flying crew inform us after take off, that it would be all right if we wanted to smoke!

That crew must have had heavy colds or the death wish but needless to add, we all refrained from indulging for the duration of that interesting flight.

Our arrival at Portreath was a source of even more dismay when we found that we were to kip down in bell-tents erected in a muddy field adjacent to the 'drome. The primitive ablution facilities were also a bit of a blow after the comparative luxury of our billets at Raynham, but at least they were no worse than that first few months in France had offered.

The dispersal areas for our Blenheims at Portreath, were right on the cliff top, with a sheer drop of 150-200 feet to the rocky shore: aerodromes are expected to be draughty places, but this was taking the fresh-air thing a bit too far; luckily it was warmish weather.

In a short while we were quite organised and had the aeroplanes all filled up and serviced, with bomb loads of A/P and Semi Armour Piercing ready for an attack next day on those two menaces in Brest harbour.

As somewhat of an award for effort, and perhaps to make us smell rather sweeter, we were offered a bath. For this experience, there was transport to a tin-mine at Redruth, to use the miners' facilities. It was well known that miners are toughies - they need to be - but that bath house proved it. The shower cubicles were cement faced brick walls about six feet high which were designed to take half a dozen men at a time. Fair enough. The shower however, came not from overhead roses, but from vertical pipes with multiple holes in, which ran up and down the walls, thus giving horizontal jets from all directions. Marvellous, you may think, but there were only two grades of temperature for these powerful jets: they must have used the exhaust from their steam pump-engine to supply the hot jets, and when the steam was off the jets became a sort of liquid ice-crystal hitting our shrinking flesh.

After this harrowing experience, it was almost essential that we went on the town before returning to camp - and camping indeed we were.

Going on the town only consisted of a few beers, and then we caught the local bus back to the village of Portreath, and from there staggered slowly up the wooded zig-zag cliff path to our 'drome on the cliffs. As luck would have it, during the climb, the sirens wailed and - just like in Norfolk, no sooner the word than the blow - Gerry was with us and from the racket ahead, had found something to drop the odd bomb on. There was no great hurry up the rest of that cliff path; bell-tents, even if one burrowed under the duck-boards, were of no great avail as air-raid shelters.

Such raids seldom lasted long, although a series of sorties may have sometimes given the effect of a continuous raid and as it quietened we got to bed. Next morning showed the result: it had been quite effective. For a start, this station had been using one of the old Cierva Autogyros as a weather kite and it was usually parked just by the watch-tower. This morning, just where the Autogyro should be was a dirty great bomb crater, and not a trace anywhere of Señor Cierva's invention. In addition, we had lost some of our Blenheims and that put paid to any raid on Brest for the foreseeable future.

It was on the cliffs at Portreath that I witnessed one of the bravest acts I ever saw. One of our bombed-up kites had stopped a piece of bomb casing shrapnel, this had passed through the side of the bomb-bay and through the sheet metal tail of one of the SAP's to bury itself into the cast-steel body of the bomb and to partly bury itself in the actual fuse of the bomb which was screwed into the rear face of the bomb. There was no way in which this fuse could be unscrewed whilst the bomb splinter remained buried alongside.

We had a Flight Sergeant Armourer with us, whose name I regret I cannot recall, but he sent everyone away as far as possible, and then, while a few of us watched from comparative safety about fifty yards away, he sat on the ground under that Blenheim and CHISELLED the splinter free, before unscrewing the fuse to make the bomb safe. As far as I know, this act was never really appreciated by general acknowledgement.

That raid with its considerable depletion to our force terminated the trip to Cornwall, and we returned to Norfolk where I found that I was to remain with the flight for the foreseeable future, and was billeted near to the ground of Oulton, at Blickling Hall - not of course, actually IN THE HALL, but in the stables thereof.

That short period of the summer of '41, while the flight was at Oulton and we were billeted in the stables of Blickling Hall was very costly in aircrew and aircraft. During it we had a series of three succeeding C/O's, but I never knew whether that was because of casualties, or more happily, because of the rapid promotions which were a part of war-time service.

One instance, as an illustration: we had a Flight Sergeant, whose name was, I seem to remember, Walsingham. In the process of under two weeks his promotion to Warrant Officer was promulgated, followed almost before he could change his stripes for the coat-of-arms badge, by his commission as Flying Officer (when W/O's were commissioned they leap-frogged the rank of Pilot Officer). With the losses of crews we were experiencing just at that time, F/O Walsingham was acting as Squadron Leader, leading on operations, and it seemed only days before he was acting Winco and our C/O. He was never actually recorded as being commanding officer, I'm sure, and life being so damned short those days, he may not have survived long enough for his rapid rise to have been perpetuated.

One day at the end of May, I walked into our flight office which was a sort of caravan at Blickling and Chiefy was just saying, "Look at that! I've got to find a corporal fitter, and send him off on a bloody DRILL course, just when we're so busy. They must be mad!"

Looking at the letter he was reviling, I saw that the course was a month-long one at Cosford. This station was only about twelve miles from my home, so I very promptly piped up, "I'll go Flight, I live near there."

"Well, you've to be there for Monday next. You can put in a weekend pass from Friday and report in there Sunday night, now get on that truck and let's have some work out of you before I change my mind!"

After filling up the Raleigh I was away on the Friday, and with a nice rest over the weekend, duly reported at Cosford on Sunday. It turned out that this course was not just a drill course, but was a kind of 'under training sergeants' course' where we were to learn not only how to drill a group of men, but all the uses of the multifarious forms and procedures in running an active flight. There was also much PT, and even a bayonet-fighting course; the net result of all this physical activity was that I became fitter then I'd ever been before or have been since.

In addition to the advantage of being near home, I discovered on that first day, that both the Warrant Officer, I/C, AND his Flight Sergeant, PTI had been in my recruits' squad at Uxbridge Depot. Needless to say, I suffered no lack of weekend passes during that month.

On return to 18 Squadron, I found that I was moved to Horsham St. Faith's which is, or was, on the outskirts of Norwich, and engaged again on larger repairs to aircraft from one or other of the operating flights. Because of this semi-isolation from the scenes of action, it was long after hostilities had ceased that I learned that 18 had been given the task of dropping a spare leg for Douglas Bader after his landing in France and capture.

One vignette comes to mind which indicated that the rest of the Squadron was still active; I was working on a Blenheim after the July 16th Rotterdam raid, when I found not one, but three well-cooked storks rammed in between the cylinders of its Mercuries. Our Blenheim pilots knew how to fly low, and only sometimes overdid it!

It had been the practice, for some time, for No. 2 Group to send one of its Blenheim squadrons out to Malta, to operate from there for a short while and then for the surviving crews and kites to fly on to the Middle East theatre, when, if the crews were lucky, they would be ferried back, sometimes by sea and sometimes, via Takoradi on the west coast of Africa and by Catalina from there.

Just how often this had occurred I don't know but when it became 18's turn, it was decided that each aircraft should carry one member of the ground staff to form a servicing nucleus in Malta. It seemed that ground staff were getting a bit thin on the ground there what with one thing or another.

Volunteers were asked for to accompany our contingent, and true to my rule that it's best to volunteer, because there's always something worse to be detailed for, I did just that. Actually, we were told that we'd be home for Christmas, and would be granted extra leave then as a reward for our voluntary efforts. Leave, too was something I could never resist.

For nearly a month after that, life was very interesting and quite exciting. We were issued with a batch of new kites, painted in the old green and brown camouflage upstairs, but the undersides were a lovely pale blue and in addition these new kites had a pair of Browning 303's hanging below the forward escape hatch in a perspex blister. They were intended for operation against an enemy attacking from under the tail, by the navigator, who was to aim and fire them using a mirror at forty-five degrees, with sights alongside the guns.

Being complete idiots, a couple of us thought it would be fun to shoot at gulls from the cliff top at Portreath, when we were servicing the aircraft there en route for Malta, and the escape hatch was lying there on the grass just tempting us. I don't know if the gulls were frightened, but the way that blistered escape hatch slid rapidly across the grass from the guns' reactive force certainly frightened me!

But that was some weeks away yet. The Squadron was still operating against the enemy, I'm sure, but for the crews of the new machines - and their fourth member in the shape of one of us normally non-flying lot - there were other things to do. Among us sixteen ground staff bods was a selection of trades, even an instrument repairer, I recall, who was reputed to be a watchmaker from Norwich. Weren't ALL RAF instrument repairers ex-watchmakers?

The gen was, that we were to fly from Cornwall to Gibraltar at 10,000 feet, which is the greatest height at which it was considered safe to fly without oxygen augmentation and then to fly down the Mediterranean as low as possible in order to avoid enemy radar from the North African coast, Tunisia, Pantellaria Island and Sicily etc.

Each leg was about on the limit of endurance for a Blenheim, so an extra tank was to be fitted in the bomb bays of the aircraft, the fuel from which would be pumped from the auxiliary tank to the main tanks in the mainplanes, by means of a small double acting 'flip-flop' pump fixed to the starboard side of the cockpit - guess who by!

In order to find the most economical engine speed and boost pressure at 10,000 and less than 50, we had to fly quite a few hours, and these hours were spent in a state of constant excitement for me. Hour after hour over England's summer countryside, dodging round buildings and woods, scaring the life out of poor farmers and then at various heights to find the most economical for the Gib run; from 3 miles or so up one can see a fair way.

But, at last, we were ready and pushed off to Portreath. This time Gerry was not to greet us so loudly, and even bell-tents didn't seem so bad. Only one night we - that is my aircraft crew and I - spent there, and we took off for the Gibraltar. Flying straight across the Bay of Biscay, after passing well to the west of Ushant, and the mountains of northern Spain were showing on the horizon after about three and a half hours. It was just then that I spotted an aircraft flying towards us on a northerly course and pointed it out to P/O Prile who was captain and pilot, thinking, "What can we do about him?" But, as it closed, it became clear that it was one of our own Blenheims, who was either lost or had decided he preferred English beer. Out of the sixteen aircraft which started from Horsham, not all reached Gibraltar, let alone Malta. One landed in Portugal, but the crew found their way home somehow, but there were others who just disappeared, which is not too surprising, as shall be related.

CHAPTER 15
Flying to Malta with 18 Squadron

As we flew on towards the Cantabrian mountains of northern Spain, it became rather warm sitting there beside P/O Prile. The cockpit area of a Blenheim is very similar to a glasshouse when the sun shines directly into it - and we were three miles nearer to it than on the deck! In addition, I was still wearing my greatcoat under the parachute harness, and pumping away with that 'flip-flop' - every pump must have put about an eggcupful into the main tanks. How previous crews had managed to find their way if the navigator had to do the pumping as well, amazes me.

Approaching Cap Finisterre, we kept well out to sea; we had been told that the Spanish were not particularly amicable to passing inglesi: but we used the coast of Portugal as a guide and followed that from about five miles out. It was quite interesting to pick out Lisbon and the mouth of the Tagus; its very sheltered land-locked harbour was very obvious from our height.

Something had to go wrong, if only slightly, but it was not until the approach to Gibraltar that we - that is I - were reminded of the perils of war-time flying. There was a rule that British aircraft should be very careful to circle around the Rock before coming in to land, and we made a circuit in the wrong direction. This took us over La Linea and Spanish territory, with the rude effect of a small salvo of Bofors tracer wending its way up towards us. Sounds slow, but that's how it seemed and luckily, either their aim was faulty, or they were only giving a warning.

On arrival at Gib, we were welcomed with a meal, and told that we could leave everything to the ground staff of the reception flight. That was probably what had been happening previously, before we took some of our people. Next morning, that is Sunday October 12th, most of the bods went to the eastern or Mediterranean side beach for a swim and general laze. It struck me however, that it might be a good idea to check up on the kites beforehand, so I put it to one of the lads, Ham Turner, who was a Fitter 1 (airframe/engine fitter), that he should check over both airframes whilst I had a good shufti around the four Mercs. This we did, and a damn good job, too. Both main and auxiliary fuel tanks of both aircraft were well short of being full, and when I recall that on arrival at Malta, there was barely enough left to circuit the 'drome it would have gone rather ill with us otherwise. But in addition, I found during my inspection, that several tappets of all four engines had worked loose during the flight from Blighty, and in one case the lock nut was missing. Needless to say, it took Ham and I most of that Sunday before we were satisfied that we'd done all we could to make sure that we lived out the week.

Those of us who were swimming in the Mediterranean also had some excitement; I heard that some of them were floating around on a sort of dinghy or raft and drifted northward until a short burst of machine-gun fire alerted them to their mistake; and probably spoilt the enjoyment of the swim somewhat.

Monday morning came, and the weekend 'holiday' being over, we re-embarked into our aircraft. We were going to takeoff easterly, because that was the direction from which the wind was blowing. In its turn, our Blenheim was taxied as far towards the harbour as was possible. After the usual run up and magneto test etc., the Mercs were wound up to full take off revs with chocks in front of the wheels and the brakes on. When Mr. Prile gave the signal, the chocks were pulled out, brakes off, and we shot across the short runway and away - at about six feet above the sea.

Nowadays, there's a runway built out into the harbour which was constructed to facilitate air operations during the 'Torch' landing but even now it must task a pilot of one of those big jets to get it clear of the deck and any shipping which is around in the harbour.

After take off, we climbed steadily to around 10,000 feet until we were well away from Gib. This was designed to fox the watching eyes over the La Linea racecourse, but it was probably a waste of fuel, because they would undoubtedly guess where we were bound, and even if they didn't guess, it was possible that someone based at Gib. would tell them. People who could be prepared to send an aircraft on a 900-plus miles over-water flight with fuel tanks insufficiently filled might well be capable of such careless talk.

The flight plan from Gibraltar to Malta was to get down as low as possible, or as low as the pilot's nerves and skill could allow, in order to keep the aircraft underneath the RADAR surveillance beams of the enemy in Tunisia, Sardinia, etc., and especially to avoid detection from the island of Pantellaria, which was reputed to be packed with Gerry and Italian fighters just waiting for nice soft targets to try to edge past. And we were certainly one of those soft targets because with the extra weight of fuel needed to complete the distance with dry feet, and an extra bod aboard - complete with the kits of four crew - there was no ammunition for the five Browning 303's we carried.

This was going to cause a little heart-stopping - at least on my part - for we were flying due east and about half-way between Bizerta in Tunisia and the island of Sardinia, when I transferred my gaze from the fascinating view of the so-close waves seen through the bomb-aimer's window in the nose, to glance out over the port engine. There I spotted a strange kite flying on the same course as ourselves, and only about 300 yards away.

Sticking out rather obviously from his dorsal cockpit was what looked to be a cannon about nine feet long. At first I thought it was an SM 79 which had a 13-7 m.m. job, but later realised that it could well have been a LeO 45, which were fitted with the 20 m.m. Hispano cannon but either would have been big enough to put US into the Mediterranean and we were only fifty feet above it already.

These Lioré et Olivier 45's were being used by both the Regia Aeronautica and the Vichy French from Tunisia at that time.

However, all was well, for P/O Prile had the answer, "Get those Brownings round and show him we're not asleep," - this to the Air Gunner in our turret, and it worked, for the LeO sheered off and we never saw him again. Either he was a very tired airman with no ammunition left, or he was just the sort of enemy one needs in such situations.

We only saw one other kite in all that longish day, and that was one of our own Blenheims who seemed to appear from nowhere - as other aircraft often do - and formatted on us, but about 200 feet above us, just as we were passing between Pantellaria and Cape Bon. The language over the radio to this high-flying gentleman from our wave-hugging pilot was quite enough to bring him down almost to our level, far enough down at least for us both to get past that very dicey area without further excitement.

It was with some relief that we rose a few thousand feet to approach the island of Malta. There would have been a rather more than enthusiastic welcome had we approached at the fifty feet height we'd maintained for the last few hours. That height gives one the full effect of one's speed: it was just like being in a fast motor-launch when looking through the bomb-aimer's window from my little folding seat beside the driver. Our approach was from the south, as we'd circled round that way to avoid being mistaken for one of those Sicilian types who were to make our lives in the near future rather less than placid. Nevertheless, it was good to see that island group, looking, as P/O Prile said as we dropped into land at Luqa aerodrome, just like a couple of bath-bricks floating in a sea of Reckitt's Blue.

Sad to relate, for he was a damned good pilot, he and the other two members of my crew failed to return to Malta after an operation less than a month after our arrival there.

The Regia Aeronautica must have heard that the redoubtable 18 Squadron was about to join the RAF in Malta, because they posted a fresh bomber group to Sicily equipped with BR 20 M's, as I heard later.

Our first mission as an offensive unit was against the seaplane base at Syracuse, when six of our Blenheims took part. There were two squadrons of Blenheims based at Luqa, and they often operated together, as also did the two squadrons of Wellingtons which were also based on Luqa. Just after our own arrival in Malta, 104 Squadron of Wimpies flew in the relieve 38 Squadron.

These were quite busy days at Luqa; we even took part in a raid as far away as Greece. 38 Squadron flew their last sorties and flew on to Shalufa in Egypt, and seven Wimpies from the U.K. took their place. It was about this time that the Naval Force "K" arrived in the theatre, of which more later. Altogether, that month of October 1941 was not a happy one - we lost thirty-five Blenheims between the two squadrons - and November wasn't much better. On the 19th, we lost three from six against an Axis convoy - but enough of that, the morbid can find all relevant details in the official histories.

There was plenty of excitement for ground crews as the war hotted up in our locality. From the northern edge of Luqa 'drome where our Blenheims were dotted about in dispersal areas, we could look down towards the harbour and town of Valetta which was about three miles away and we could also see the 'drome at Takali from whence operated the two squadrons of Hurricane One day fighters and the few night-fighter Hurricanes we had then. The famous Gladiators had long since gone the way of all gladiators. As a consequence of this grandstand view (and the habit the enemy had of concentrating any one raid on a particular target), unless we were that target, we could just stand and watch with a weather eye open for the odd rogue. In the first month or so, the Regia Aeronautica usually came in very high with escorting Macchi 202's actually in formation, above them; but, towards December, our old 'friends' the Luftwaffe, came to Sicily for their winter break from the hardships of the Russian campaign; and they were a different kettle of fish.

Working on an aircraft one day, and this was during an alert (because the orders were that shelter should only be sought when the aerodrome was actually under direct attack) there was a sudden flurry and a Junkers 88 flew across skimming the grass, with not one but two Hurribirds on his tail; that was one that didn't return for his bottle of Marsala.

On another occasion, Ham Turner and I were working on a kite at dispersal with one eye on the sky, for this too was during an alert and the flak was flying although Luqa wasn't that time under attack. Suddenly there was that sound of a bomb descending rapidly, and we dived into a shallow trench which was alongside the tent in which we kept our tools and spare spark plugs etc. There was an ear-splitting clang and when we investigated, we saw that a damn Bofors shell which had failed to explode in the air had landed right on the fuselage of the Blenheim just in front of the tail-unit. And it had not failed to explode then! The nose-cap was buried under the kite and the fuselage looked a bit like a pepper pot - the tail unit of a Blenheim is attached by means of a ring of what seems like hundreds of 4 BA screws with captive nuts, and it was quite a job to repair.

Just below our dispersal points the land had been terraced by Maltese farmers, and at odd intervals one could find bottle-shaped holes which had been dug as wells to collect water for irrigation, etc. There are no streams running on Malta. The whole island is limestone similar to Cotswold stone, and rain just disappears underground. These bottle-wells were quite handy as air-raid shelters, and we had one near us, to which we had fixed a knotted rope for sliding down there quick when real necessity drove us, and the damaged and very ragged looking main spar from a Wimpy as a ladder for regaining the world of light and fresh air. Those wells were absolutely claustrophobic to me and it was much better to duck behind sandbags etc., than risk what seemed like a premature burial!

Much to be preferred as an underground shelter was a natural cave which ran from a valley running near to our end of the 'drome, but this needed some earlier warning of need before high-tailing towards it. However, a few of us did venture there on one time when Gerry became too personal and we were happily resting in the depths of the cave when a Maltese goatherd decided that he would like to join us - and brought his charges with him. If the reader has ever been in close proximity to a herd of goats in an enclosed space, they will readily understand why we left the shelter of the cave and took our chance with any unfriendly action Gerry might take.

In December, the 19th, I think, 40 Squadron had some ill-luck. One of their Wimpies was being serviced after an operation the night before, when it seems that an armourer, in inspecting the bomb bay, failed to notice that one of the forty pounders had been left just resting on the bomb doors. These are returned by means of bungee elastic ropes after bomb release, and were apparently just strong enough to sustain the weight of that bomb. When the armourer pulled down the bomb door, out dropped the forty pounder, and its explosion was fatal to several of the erks around the kite. In addition, the subsequent fire destroyed two other Wimpies, one of which was loaded with a 4000 pounder.

Just before Christmas, 107's Blenheims attacked a convoy on the road west of Sirte, in Libya. One of them was unfortunately lost, and another hit a Gerry ammo or fuel truck, which blew up just as he was above it. The resulting loosening of the rivets in that Blenheim made it a real miracle that he came safely back to Malta. The kite sounded like a tin of marbles if one shook it!

The most devastating raid on Luqa whilst 18 was there occurred just after Christmas, the 29th I think. Nine Wimpies were written off in that raid, six of them part of a new delivery in transit through the island, and three of 40 Squadron. As the latter were burning well and were adjacent to the main bomb dump, there was a general nervousness around; anyone not immediately required for duty was advised to leave camp for safer areas. The dump was not actually destroyed, I believe, but from the noises coming from around the Safi strip region, a fair amount of amatol must have been destabilised.

Ham Turner and I decided that Valetta might be a preferential area, and we lost little time in getting there. When the time came to return to Luqa, we decided to stay at an hotel in Valetta which seemed a good idea at the time! We booked in at a hotel in Strada Reale (King Street), and were shown down some stairs to a room with two iron framed beds and a marble floor. There was a window frame, but it was closed by wooden shutters. As we'd walked down from the street, we thought, "Well, we'll be fairly safe down here. That must be one of those windows into an area to give ventilation, etc."

Settling down for the night, we were quite soon awakened by sirens, but apart from slipping a few clothes on, we stayed put despite hearing loud bangs in the near distance. It was when we heard that unmistakable crackling of burning timbers, that we decided to investigate via the area shutters. A nasty shock awaited us; the window did not open to an area, but straight to the harbour, and we were not as we had supposed, some floors down, but were on the top floor and the building next door was burning furiously! To quote the bible, we waited not upon the order of our going, but scampered very smartly. Back in King Street, we made our way to the communal shelter with our Maltese friends and there spent the rest of the night. We forgot to ask the hotel for a refund, but they might perhaps have refused anyway.

The Force 'K' I mentioned earlier as arriving in the Malta area of operations consisted of two six-inch cruisers, the Penelope and Aurora, together with Ajax of River Plate fame, and Neptune. Of these ships, HMS Penelope was, we were told, due for a refit in Blighty before Christmas: and when those aircraft and aircrews which were still serviceable flew on to the Middle East, we, the lucky ground crew 'passengers', would be getting a lift home in Penelope.

Unfortunately, on December 18th, whilst operating off the coast of Tripoli, Force 'K' ran into a minefield. HMS Neptune went to join her namesake the Sea God, Aurora was severely damaged, and although Penelope was only slightly damaged she could not now be spared from the Mediterranean. So disappeared our proposed lift home, and most of us now resigned ourselves to soldiering on with fairly good grace.

As if to counter our resignation, life at Luqa became more and more hectic as the Luftwaffe increased their activities over the island, and most nights were spent in deep shelters as the norm. This saved the discomfort of moving from the billet to shelter when a not-infrequent raid occurred.

It was during these long periods under about twenty feet of Maltese limestone that I, and a couple of others, were taught to play Contract Bridge by Johnny Saunders, a Welsh lad who had been a teacher prior to joining the RAF.

Because Malta obtained its water from underground, well-cutting was a local skill. The vast majority of the buildings of the island were of their free-cutting limestone, so there was a plentiful supply of stonemasons who turned their hands to shelter construction as the need arose. Their method was to drill a well shaft some three to four feet in diameter vertically downward, then to cut horizontally a 'cave' or a tunnel some six to seven feet high and about the same wide, and then to work their way back to the surface by cutting steps through a ninety degree turn, finishing off with an entrance at surface level, surrounded by nice large lumps of solid rock.

It was a bit cool down there after an hour or so, and a peculiarity of the limestone strata often gave the impression that bombs falling some distance away were about two feet away, while near misses sometimes sounded miles away; it all made life quite interesting.

To the reader it may seem that we were fairly often in fear of our lives, but strangely it wasn't like that for much of the time; there were some very interesting places to visit when the opportunity offered - a lace factory was still operating and one could buy work there, as also was a pipe factory. The briarwood raw material came from North Africa we were told. There was a cinema in Valetta, which was reputed to be the oldest theatre in Europe. It was built in the round, Shakespearean fashion, with many tiers of boxes and a central stage. To use it as a cinema, a screen had been erected in front of some boxes, which gave a very funny aspect to the picture if one sat too close to the side of the screen. I only went there once, when I saw a film called 'The North West Passage' in which a Gatling Gun was fired: it was difficult to decide whether the firing was coming from the screen - or outside in Valetta!

One day wandering around Valetta, I noticed a revolver for sale in a secondhand shop, and thought it a good idea to have some personal means of propagating the war effort. It had a very short barrel and practising on the fleshy leaves of prickly pear cactuses showed that it was not very accurate but it did have the great advantage that it accepted the same ammunition as the issue Enfield revolvers.

Despite the increasing offensiveness of Gerry, there was a period of nearly a week at the beginning of December which was almost raid-free. We put this down to the fact that a couple of Beaufighters of 252 Squadron had dropped in on a visit and been persuaded to give a hand and a surprise to the Luftwaffe before returning to their base in North Africa. Entertainingly, Form 252 was the reference of a Charge Sheet in the RAF, but the little intermission did not last; thereafter raids increased in number and intensity, and our own (i.e. Luqa's) offensive action was also increased with concomitant losses of aircraft and, sadly, aircrews.

I've read since, in other wartime accounts, that Gerry left us alone on Christmas Day, but I distinctly remember that whilst we were queuing outside the dining hut for our Christmas dinners, a 109 flew across the 'drome and in between the stone-built huts of the living quarters to liven us up a little!

New Year's Day gave us a bit of a lift when we learned that 21 Squadron, another 2 Group Blenheim squadron, were leaving England to join (or possibly relieve) us in Malta.

With the two Wimpy squadrons operating from Luqa at night, activity in the dark hours was about the same as in daylight. I remember one night - how could it be forgotten? - when one, or it may have been several, cheeky Gerries followed the Wimpies home after an operation, and every time the Chance Light lit up the runway, dropped a bomb or so on the runway. A gang of us were turfed out into the cold wet night to fill in the craters as quickly as possible in between landing approaches of the Wellingtons and the bombing runs of what sounded like 88's. Not to be recommended as a health cure this, but we won that little action of attrition by having more shovels than Fritz had bombs, and all the Wimpies managed to land fairly safely.

Our reprieve was also at hand, for Wingco Smythe pulled one out of the hat and flew out of Luqa for Egypt with five of our kites on January 10th to be followed a couple of days later by the other flight-commander with a further five aircraft.

This exodus left only two U/S Blenheims at Luqa: it also left a Sgt Pilot Davies, his navigator and the airgunner wireless operator and another aircrew. Their instructions were to fly on these remnant

Blenheims if or when they had been made serviceable and airworthy. It also left Ham Turner and myself the unenviable task of making these kites serviceable on an aerodrome which was being subjected to an increasing number of what seemed like personal attacks on Ham and me. My diary tells me that there were thirteen separate raids on Luqa on January 13th.

One of these two aircraft, I know, needed a complete ignition harness change at least, and the other one had damage to the control cables; it was probably the one which had taken delivery of that descending Bofors round. The sum total was quite a bit of work for the two of us, but we completed it to our satisfaction by the evening of the 14th January and now came the bitter bit as the song has it - one of the kites was nice and handy for the end of the runway, but the other had been on a softish dispersal point and had sunk well in to the deck.

After running up the engines for their final check, it proved about immovable when I attempted to taxi it up on to the perimeter track, and it was by now almost dusk. With Ham on the tail to assist in keeping that down, I took both engines up to nine pounds take off boost pressure. But the kite only rocked about and still refused to come unstuck, so with both engines on full throttle, I put the airscrews into coarse pitch - which is NOT to be recommended usually - and she shot out of the mud and up onto the peritrack like a scalded cat, with Hammy holding on tight and being bashed about a bit. Quite an exciting moment or two that. It was only some thirty feet to the peritrack, and that was only just wide enough to take the width of the undercart so, as the kite leapt out of its little nest, I had to put the rudder hard over to the starboard and apply full brake to that wheel. It gave Ham a rough ride for a second but we ended up facing the right way and on hard ground, it only remained now to taxi up alongside the other kite, get our kit packed and aboard, inform Sgt Davies and the other fly-boys, and pray that the bloody Luftwaffe didn't come and write-off our last chance.

Well, they didn't, and the eight of us were on the dispersal area at the crack of dawn - or soon after - but were prevented from taking off by those types from Sicily on two occasions. We finally took off at 10.15 a.m. and even then it was touch and go with a red warning on; both aircraft were moving off in takeoff mode when the watch tower gave us a red Verey light which meant abort.

"Go for it now, or we'll never get off this bombing range," I shouted at the driver, so both kites ignored the signal and away we went.

Despite having taken off during a raid, we never actually saw any other aircraft but our companion Blenheim all the way to the Egyptian coast, where we landed at Fuka because of failing daylight and lack of fuel.

There, we were made reasonably welcome, given a good meal after parking the aircraft on the landing ground, and kipped down for the night in a tent. We slept for ten hours that night with absolutely no interruptions from any other air force, Gerry, Iti or Chinese, and after breakfast and a quick check over the kites, when we found that a total of five pieces of AA debris had hit us during the takeoff from Luqa, took a short hop over to Fuka satellite for juice. But they were either short of petrol or just mean, and sent us back a few miles westward to Bagouch from whence we followed the railway most of the way to Cairo, where we landed at Heluan about 1500 hours.

CHAPTER 16
Escape from Malta - to Cairo and the W. Desert

Our little flight of two Blenheim 'escapologists' landed happily and safely in the Delta at Almaza, a RAF camp and airfield in the oasis of Heluan. This place was not, as the term 'oasis' may imply to readers of 'Beau Geste', just a muddy pool and a few date palms, but it was a fairly substantial small town lying about ten miles south of Cairo of which it is really a suburb, and connected by a modern (then) diesel-engined railway, the rails of which were continuously welded to give a very smooth ride; a method not found in dear old Blighty for some years after the war.

After seeing to the well-being of the aircraft, we gathered our kit, such as it was, and were transported by truck into Cairo where we found to our delight that we were being billeted in an hotel.

The hotel, in Shari Emad ed Din, was known as Jolley's, owned perhaps by an expatriate of that name, and they fed us like princes; three-course lunches (or tiffins, using the usual RAF-adopted Indian word for the midday meal) and full four-course dinners. This was like heaven after the monotonous meals of tinned bacon with captured Iti macaroni which had appeared so often on the Luqa menus.

Next day, a Saturday, I fixed up an advance of pay in this new currency of 100 piastres to the pound Egyptian (£E), and the eight of us, the two aircrews with Ham and I, decided that we should do the 'tourist thing' and see the famous Pyramids. There were several ways of getting to Giza, one could take a taxi and a dragoman or guide but the way we travelled was by tram, the Number 14 tram, and 1½ piastres each took us the whole way several miles out into desert areas beyond the Nile. The Sphinx, at that time, was just in process of having much of the drifted sand overburden removed to expose the basaltic temple behind the famous head. It might have been better for the Sphinx had it been left buried, when one considers the effects of the last fifty years' exposure to the wind-driven sands and the curiosity-driven feet of tourists.

We had been told before leaving Norfolk for Malta, that we shouldn't inform our folks about our future destination, and that had made sense to most of us, so we spent that first Sunday in writing letters home, but the tourism began again on Monday.

There couldn't have been any situation like ours before, in any war or peace time; for a group of mixed senior and junior NCO's to be billeted in a fairly expensive hotel at Air Force expense, and no duties, it was a dream from which we must surely be awakened soon. Nevertheless, another tram ride, this time at the prodigious expense of 5 milliemes - i.e. ½ piastre - to Cairo Zoo. This well-managed institution was organised somewhat on the lines of Whipsnade, but with the extra interest of trees from all around the world growing among the animal enclosures, and each tree identified with its name in English and Latin and place of origin.

Then on the next day, we all visited a couple of Cairo's many mosques and finished the day with a concert of classical music at an establishment which must have been under the auspices of ENSA and the NAAFI, called 'Music For All'.

January 1st saw us at Heluan, where we received an issue of khaki battledress but after only a short work session on our aircraft, we were back to the flesh-pots of Le Caire and that evening we heard a violin recital by a young lad of fifteen, Joseph Segar.

But this was the day when Erwin von Rommel began to get rough from the position at El Agheila to which Wavell had driven him; a day that was fated to have an effect on our immediate and distant futures if we had but known.

As if to underline this, on the very next day, not only was there an air-raid alert at Almaza, when the deep shelters of Malta were remembered with some affection, but we also flew four of our Blenheims off to El Fayoum, another airfield further south.

The war still remained just something one read about in the papers, the food remained just as appetising; and to cap all, I discovered that the New Zealand Forces had a Service Club where one could get a hot bath, and so I enjoyed something I'd not had for over four months.

Nothing lasts forever, and on February 5th I was aroused from my bed in Jolley's at 4.30 a.m., breakfasted at 5.00 a.m., and was taking-off from El Fayoum at 8.30 a.m. After an hour or so of looking down at practically featureless desert sand, we landed at a small landing ground near Sidi Barrani.

One certainly experienced rapid changes of living conditions in wartime service; the extremes would be difficult to realise without having been exposed to such vicissitudes. There were many campaigns in my, and the other earlier, contest much more demanding than my own: I sometimes wonder just how those bods felt and reacted in their muddy shell holes and trenches of the '14-18 effort, with the constant thought that at any minute their life would end with a bang; and the lads of the jungle fighting against that other foe, with leeches and high humidity as extras.

At least we in the desert campaign were reasonably dry, and at Sidi Barrani we had better food than when in Blighty: goodness knows how the cooks managed it.

As soon as the kites were serviced after landing, we looked around in the time-honoured manner for a cushy billet. There were ridge tents available, and a couple of us found the remnants of an old dugout and began to clear it of drift sand and old tins, beer bottles etc. after which we erected a seven foot by seven foot ridge over it so that we were sheltered from dust and rain - it often rained along the coastal strip - and of course, the odd bit of bomb splinter which might be directed our way. The rest of the troops arrived by lorry two days later, and we two were much more comfortably housed by then than they were going to have time to organise.

Two of the Blenheims were almost immediately sent off to operate from an airfield near Benghazi, but found, as they attempted to land there, that Gerry considered it to be a private Luftwaffe Only field. Rommel had ridden in to Benghazi nearly a week before - somebody might have told us! But if they had not been so trigger-happy, the Luftwaffe could have gained a couple of nice serviceable Blenheims. War-time is one long history of mistakes and pure luck.

The desert road ran near this landing ground - LG 05 - and one day two German light armoured vehicles, with each a NZ driver, called in and tried to skive a tankful of petrol each.

"Sorry, our petrol is special aviation fuel, and we need all we have for the aircraft," we told them. Without further ado, these two Antipodean squaddies just dumped their mounts with us and hitched lifts eastwards towards the Delta.

"There go a couple of keen types," we thought. "If they're not deserters, they must be Rommel's advance party."

It was not all bad however, because instead of having to taxi the kites to our petrol bowser, we could now tow the bowser to the aeroplanes by using one of these light Gerry tanks.

One slight disadvantage about them was that they had boxes of those little red Italian hand-grenades on board, and one day when we were down on the shore washing the sand out of our hair and ears, some fool thought it would be fun to see if he could kill some fish with them. Unfortunately, only one actually detonated, and our swimming spot was rendered much less attractive by having fused and unexploded grenades lying around to catch the toe on!

It was on one of these swimming trips at Sidi Barrani, that I spotted an adder sleeping and minding its own business in the corner of a wrecked house near the shore. From about ten feet I drew a bead on it with the .38 which I'd bought in Valletta, and actually hit it, not once, but in three places, because it had been curled up. For a joke, I placed the defunct reptile very artistically draped over the front wing of the three-tonner in which we had ridden to the beach but when Flight Sergeant Rainer, our Chiefy, stepped into the cab, he never even noticed it, so it was a good job it was well dead!

With our lads losing ground to Rommel, it began to look a bit unhealthy as he moved his Stukas and such eastwards, so that on the 14th we saw off our kites and left by road ourselves in the two three-tonners by 10.45 a.m. and arrived road-weary and thirsty about four in the afternoon at Fuka, another of those semi-permanent landing ground of the Western Desert.

After erecting our tents and having a meal - cooked by bods already at Fuka, another remnant of a Blenheim squadron - we stayed in the E.P.I.P dining-cum-canteen tent, drinking bottled Canadian beer until about 10.30 p.m.

The Canadian Government must have had a very sympathetic understanding of the need their troops in the Western Desert would have to keep their body fluids at a healthy level. Not only did the desert seem awash with that lovely Black Horse, but the beer itself had the kick of a horse. The most comparable drinks were the Lion Beer of the South African Air Force, and export Guinness which was sometimes available in some Cairo bars.

It often seemed to me that there were more Commonwealth troops in the desert Air Forces than there were RAF types and when one thinks of how successive governments have treated our Empire since, I should be very surprised if they backed us up to the same extent should the need ever arise again. Had the Empire remained as a REAL Commonwealth, there would have been no need for all this mixing with the Europeans, just to expedite trade with them; we lost a great deal more trade with our Dominions than we gained nearer home when we drove them to deal with other nations. But enough, it's too late now to turn the clock back.

For the next three or four days at Fuka, nothing very exciting seemed to be happening; we serviced the kites as necessary, and two or three of them flew off westwards each day and obviously something was going on but it wasn't considered necessary to tell us groundlings what it was. Subsequent gen was that Rommel was stirring things up a bit - including the surface of the earth.

Something certainly happened on our fifth day at Fuka, when we awoke to find the air moving at about fifty miles per hour and bringing the desert with it! As the kites had returned from wherever they had been, during a lull in the storm, that afternoon was spent in giving the machines a good check over. And the next day was very similar; I recall helping to change a wheel during the blow, and that sandstorm was a bit unusual in that it was raining at the same time, so that the wind spread a sort of light brown mud over everything, and everybody.

Reading in the tent with a sandstorm blowing was very annoying; as the sand hit the canvas of the tent it was filtered and a fine rain of gritty powder kept obscuring the pages, almost as fast as one could brush it away.

The aircraft usually took off in line abreast, so that they didn't fill each other's air-intakes with the resultant sand-lift but even so, their air filters quickly became clogged, with considerable effect on their mixture control so it was a major part of a daily inspection to see that the filters were clean. This meant removal, washing the element in petrol, then soaking it in oil, and re-fitting. After doing this sort of job, one only wanted to get down to the sea and have a good soak oneself.

Consistent with the exigencies of the Service, as the official phrase put it, we visited the beach as often as we could. Water for personal ablutions was fairly scarce - it was not unknown for erks to shave in half-mugs of valuable tea, after drinking the first half.

Odd finds were made on that coastal strip; one day we found the beach littered with hundreds of oranges, none of which to our chagrin proved to be edible after their saltwater immersion. Somebody went short of a supply of vitamin C when THAT ship was sunk. Another find was a tin about one foot high by eight inches in diameter, which we were a bit wary of because of the possibility of booby traps. Our rather devious enemies had a habit of making apparently innocuous objects surprisingly deadly, as no doubt did we ourselves when the opportunity arose.

However, after careful examination and much thought we decided to attack this can, but it proved to contain nothing more harmful than good old beef dripping. Taken in conjunction with the odd eggs which were often available from the mysterious source of 'local' children, the dripping made a welcome addition to our diet.

One of the quite amazing and still baffling aspects of desert life was the origins of these eggs. One might be sitting in or near one's tent when a voice literally 'out of the blue' would say, "Eggis Effendi?" and a little Arab lad would be standing there with a basket of eggs, and sometimes even tomatoes. We, or at least I, never found out where these children lived, where the food was grown - or how, or where the hens were kept. Sometimes they would accept cigarettes as payment in lieu of ackers (piastres), but they had to be well-known brands, as even the Arabs wouldn't smoke the rubbish which was issued to the troops under the inappropriate name of 'Victory'.

A rather more intriguing find was a smaller tin, this one only a couple of inches deep and three to four inches in diameter. It had a press-in lid, which it took a great deal of foolhardy courage to prise off, to find the contents still sealed by what felt like a thin metal filament. That had to be pierced, but when consuming curiosity finally overcame fear and common sense, there was revealed a brown powder. "Hm," we thought, "dried blood, containing some new virus disease perhaps."

"Smells like coffee!" I dipped a finger in, and tasted it. "It is coffee." That must have been everybody's introduction to a wonder of the future, Nestlé's instant dried coffee powder.

The day we found the boat was intriguing: the boat was small, only about eight feet long, lying on the sand as if someone had just drawn it up from the water, and it was a perfect example of the sort of craft which a large yacht would use around the harbour - clinker-built mahogany and varnished so that it shone in the sun. It seemed a pity to leave it there, but what could we do with it?

Not far away along the shore we came upon a bundle of wood, or so at first sight it appeared to be. There was an oar, and of all things, a length of ordinary builder's ladder, together with odd pieces of timber and planking all lashed together with copper wire. But it was what was lashed to this construction that rocked us a bit. It was a human torso, just that - no arms, no legs, no head - and certainly no clothing. How this man had managed to lash himself to his makeshift raft with the copper wire still intrigues me, for the wire was from the armature of an electric motor - and that armature was still there, on the end of the wire.

I regret that we failed to give him a decent burial, but perhaps someone did that for him later.

Gerry must have moved quite a bit closer to us by 26th February, because we had a stick of incendiaries dropped near us that night, they didn't do the sand much harm, but it was a hint. Taking the hint seriously, we spent not a little time in digging out a slit trench beside the tent next morning, and it proved to be no time-waster even though we met an iron-pan of three to four inches thick just about a foot down, which needed a hammer and chisel to break through.

On that lovely sunny morning of February 27th, we were watching a long munitions train chugging along the railway, which ran about a mile and a half or so to the south of us when it was attacked by a Gerry kite, and a hit set a couple or so of its trucks alight. As we stood there, the army crew of the train stopped her, and unhooking those flaming trucks and the ones behind them, drew away with the major portion of their charge safely, so that at least most of the munitions aboard were salvaged for our lads on the sharp end to use.

That must have taken real devotion to duty, and the sort of guts which wins battles - if not wars. Our own C/O, Wingco Smythe, seemed to me to have that sort of courage; when he had been leading a Flight of Blenheims from Malta on one of those low-level attacks on Rommel's supply shipping, the other crews had told us of how he usually went in first with his bombing run, and then stooged around the target to draw its fire whilst the rest of the Flight made their low-level runs. One day he had come home (if Luqa could be called that) with a hole in one mainplane through which one could have passed a fifty gallon oil drum.

March 5th saw my machine flying up to Barrani which meant that tomorrow it would need a really good going over.

That afternoon we had some excitement - a Junkers 88 had the impudence to stooge around the 'drome for nearly an hour at between three thousand and zero feet. Only the day before a battery of Bofors light AA which had been our ground defence had moved off elsewhere, so as far as we could tell, all we had to deal with him was a Lewis gun which a couple of armourers, who lived in the tent just behind mine, had rigged up on its flimsy tripod. There WAS something else, as shall be shown.

This 88 just flew around, dropping the odd bomb as he thought fit, having a little target practice, and generally giving us the jitters. A very unfortunate Albacore, which made its last mistake by flying past the airfield on its way to the Delta, got a very nasty surprise when the 88 flew alongside it, and just shot it out of the sky. There were seven bods in that kite we discovered, who were probably cadging a lift for a spot of leave in Cairo; they must have felt pretty helpless crammed in the rear cockpit, when the Junkers opened up.

Retribution was to follow: at Fuka, there was a system of defence known as P.A.C. This ingenious idea consisted of rows of rockets, which could be fired in lines across the front of low level attacking aircraft, from a static and, in this case, nicely sandbagged position. The rockets ascended to some 500 feet, carrying with them a light steel cable, at the extent of the cable, a small parachute opened which supported the cable as it slowly descended. Our unwelcome visitor took slight exception to our two friends with the Lewis and turned towards our end of the 'drome at some 400 or so feet. It so happened that he was headed directly for one of the batteries of P.A.C. and what was more, the erk with the finger on the buttons was awake. Up went the rockets, right in front of the 88, and up also went the Junkers to try to climb over them. This gave that bright pair with the Lewis a chance to get off nearly a full drum right where it would hurt most - and it must have, because he flew off towards the sea and we heard later, because the air gunner was picked up from the sea, that the pilot had been hit and mortally wounded. Fireworks do, sometimes, justify their existence!

After our experience of semi-helplessness of the day before, a couple of us decided that something must be done to alter that. But before doing anything like that, my aircraft had need of attention after its flight to Barrani and back, and it was fairly unpleasant work with a bit of dust-storm blowing.

Nevertheless, there being a kite with a main wheel needing to be changed, I removed one of the Brownings from its turret and attempted to devise a Heath Robinson mounting for it near to our tents. This was done by using a Lewis mounting slightly modified, which could well be compared to the sort of music stand which violinists use - very spindly, but better than nothing. Having managed to fit the gun in such a fashion that it could be moved around and up and down, fitted a cartridge belt container to dangle below, fastened with soft iron wire to the Lewis stand upright, and wired a piece of broomstick alongside the breech, which, tucked under the left arm, gave some measure of control, it only remained to invent a trigger. These guns were of course, fired by compressed-air means in the turret, and that would have been difficult, but I discovered that a cartridge pushed into the 'works' released the bolt once the gun was cocked - and away it went... By using my issue jack-knife can-opener tool instead, the action was much more positive.

There was one small snag: during a test firing across the landing ground, the gun more or less decided for itself where it was going to send its shots, and the resultant spray upset someone, because the message came soon after that its use should be confined to action against the enemy as and when it was necessary.

Disappointingly, it never did become necessary; possibly because by mid-February Rommel's advance had been stopped at Gazala and both sides were consolidating their positions. By the 15th, I found that I had to dismount the Browning and refit it into its Blenheim and then help in changing both its main undercarriage wheel and the tail wheel: very rough some of these landing grounds were, with all sorts of debris lying around apart from the rockery.

On the 21st all our faint hopes of being sent home were finally dashed as we were told that the Squadron out here was now disbanded, and we were going back to the Delta. Leaving Fuka at 7.30 a.m. in our 3-tonners, we arrived at Helouan about five, and most of us promptly jumped on the diesel train for Bab-el-Louk station in Cairo where I had a bath and a much-needed haircut in the New Zealand Club.

CHAPTER 17
Mm.E.F. and the Egyptian Air Force.

After a couple of days in the flesh-pots of Le Caire, I reported to an MU - No 111. This unit was part of the massive backup in the Delta to the actual fighting strength of the Desert Air Force. Here we took in salvaged engines and after complete overhauling, tested and sent them out to the squadrons.

The workshops were in large caves cut into the limestone of the Mokattam Hills which run more or less parallel to the Nile southwards from Cairo. It was from these caverns that the rock from which the Pyramids were constructed was quarried. A peculiarity of the place was that the entrances to the caves were not at the valley floor, but some way up the cliffs of the hills. At some time in the past, a roadway had been terraced around the cliff face to connect most of the cave entrances. It was, however, a long way round to get to some of these entrances, and so the RAF (one presumes) decided to erect one straight road from near the railway to connect with the terraced one.

To watch this being done day by day, gave a splendid insight into the means by which the Pyramids themselves were erected. A multitude - literally - of Egyptian fellaheen walked along the site of the road and when told where, emptied the basketload of rock and sand which they were carrying. There were men AND WOMEN carrying baskets, there were young children with donkeys, men with camels, all walking towards the hills loaded, and walking away to refill their baskets. In a remarkably short time, the road rose ramp-like to reach the upper terraced road, and we had a new approach to the caverns along which trucks could run on a tarmacked surface; almost unbelievable.

One of these caves was used for storing engines in their transport cases and was known as the Cathedral Cave, not without reason. There was even a fully equipped hospital in one cave but my place of work when I joined 111 MU was in the R.R. Merlin workshop. Although the work was interesting in itself I was in charge of an assembly bay fitting cylinders to Merlins; the very monotony of doing much the same job over and over again began to bore me and it was with relief that I agreed to move out into the desert environs to the test benches. Noisy it may have been there, and certainly much better than in those coolish caverns but the concrete floors of those caves were the home of countless fleas, to combat which the first job each morning had been to pour Keatings' Powder down inside the stockings and then watch the little fellows popping out and leaping gaily away.

The work at the test benches was as much a test of us as of the engines, but more satisfying than underneath those hills. We tested a few Bristol Hercules sleeve-valve engines, and we had a bench fitted to take the Allison engines of the Kittyhawks. For the Merlins we had properly calibrated fans to fit instead of airscrews, but for the Allisons we used Curtiss electric airscrews and adjusted their pitch to give a reasonable result. One odd thing I noticed about these fans: when I walked across in front of a bench with an Allison running, the vibrations often synchronised with my diaphragm and it was agony, but neither the Merlins nor the Hercules fans had that effect.

We worked twenty-four hours a day there in three shifts, and it was quite difficult to sleep in the daytime when on night shift from 11 to 7 a.m. I shared a big E.P.I.P. tent with another Corporal, who had been a tester at Rolls, Derby, and one day we were together in a bar in Helouan, and got into conversation with a Swedish gentleman who, we understood, was the owner of the big cement works at Tura-el-Asmant, quite close to our MU, in fact used the same station of the Cairo-Helouan railway. This obviously wealthy bod invited us to visit his house and to use his swimming pool whenever we were off duty. Naturally, we took him up on this and having found his dwelling, hidden behind fifteen feet high walls, we were led by an Egyptian servant fellow, through gardens which could have been in Surrey, to a swimming pool surrounded by lawns. As we were cooling off in the water, he came out with a tray of iced water melon for our delectation; such luxury couldn't last. With working long hours, little sleep and swimming when I should have been resting, I developed pneumonia, and after one night in the hospital cave, was transferred to the New Zealand General Hospital at Helouan, where I remained for nearly a month. The NZ Forces had a convalescent camp at Nathanya on the coast of Palestine, and to there I was dispatched when leaving dock.

But life did not remain so pleasant on arrival: British authorities made the decision that not being a Kiwi, even though I WAS a non-flying type, I must go to an Army con depot. Very funny ideas these army types had about what was convalescence. After sleeping on the beach that first night because the hut they put me in was alive with bedbugs, they thought it good medicine to have us running around the camp on PT before breakfast. After breakfast, it was gardening fatigues! I saw the M.O. there and informed him that if I was fit enough for that I was fit enough to do my job back in the Delta, so why not send me back there.

This remark had little immediate effect except to make me a bit unpopular with the local medico but at least I was excused all that PT and gardening for the remainder of my stay with the 'brown jobs'. Their idea of gardening was the usual one of whitewashing stones along the borders of all roads within the camp, and cutting any grass which showed signs of wanting to grow above an inch.

I was at Nathanya for ten days before I managed to get a casual pay parade, so found walking around the area a good way of passing time and getting fit at the same time. It was a small Jewish settlement, the main means of whose subsistence seemed to be the products of the many small citrus orchards around.

I discovered one day a large hut from which military music emanated and on investigating, found it occupied by the band of my old Territorial mob, the Staffs. Yeomanry, doing a spot of practice. Apparently, they were in the area ostensibly looking after the regimental horses at an adjacent remount depot. When I told them that I was ex-Yeomanry and suggested that a bit of equestrian exercise would do me good, they laughed and said I could borrow the necessary saddlery and any horse I fancied at any time. Snag was, they continued, that the mounts for the most part had not been ridden since the regiment had arrived in the Middle East, because as soon as they landed, the regiment had been re-equipped with armoured cars and light tanks, to help dislodge the Vichy French from Syria. As that was nearly three years since, and I was in no fit condition for a spot of horse-wrangling, I gave up the idea of seeing Palestine from the saddle. Just as well for, sometime later, I hired a horse from a livery stable at Heliopolis and, making the mistake of telling the Scots proprietor that I could ride, was given a lively steed that promptly threw me off - and that sandy paddock was hard.

With a few pounds in my pocket, I could range farther afield and hitch-hiked into Jerusalem, partly on an Arab bus with some fifty or so other folk over sixty miles of hilly country which included a winding road called, for obvious reasons, the Seven Sisters. In

Jerusalem, I stayed at the YMCA, which incidentally, was the St. David's Hotel, later to be bombed by Haganah or the other lot, Irgun Zvai Lumi.

At the St David's, I met an old shipmate from HMS FURIOUS days, and together we toured the old city, including the Dome of the Rock, the Church of the Nativity, Gethsemane and I took my life in my hands and wandered around in the narrow streets behind St. David's. One thing which I found surprising was the complete blackout at night; one almost needed to feel one's way by hand - this was a great contrast to Cairo, where the nights were ablaze with lights. Cairo, of course, was a special case - it was generally believed among the troops - that we had an agreement with Mussolini and the Luftwaffe that if they left Cairo and the Gezira Cricket Club unbombed then we would not interfere with their pleasures in Rome.

The next day after my interlude in Jerusalem found me back in the family at the RAF Rest Camp, Tel Aviv, in the suburbs of the city and right on the beach; not only on the beach, but, unlike the Army Convalescent Camp, here the huts were clean and free from bedbugs.

Tel Aviv at that time was very similar to an English seaside town: one could stroll along the front in the evening, and buy corn-on-the-cob from barrows like our own hot chestnut stands. This maize, which was soaked in butter and with a little salt, was delicious. One could also eye the local girls as one walked along, and with about the same success as one had in Margate. Nil!

I see from my diary that on September 19th I went over to Ramleh to see some of the old Squadron who were stationed there, and, on returning to Tel Aviv, found that a party of us were leaving for Cairo at 1400 hours. One shouldn't complain I suppose, but the train was crowded, the seats were hard wooden slatted ones, and we didn't arrive at the Bab-el-Hadid station until 9.30 a.m. the next day. Not surprisingly, I visited the New Zealand Club for a shower and a good meal before reporting back to my Unit at Tura.

Next day was a really special one. Reporting sick as is usual after leaving hospital, I was granted seven days' sick leave. There were three letters from my mother awaiting me, and to cap it all, I found that my third stripe had at last caught up with me.

Booking in at Jolley's Hotel in Cairo, as a base for what turned out to be another round of tourism, I met Johnny Saunders, and with him paid another visit to the Pyramids, and joined a YMCA tour to the

Delta Barrages, where the Egyptians take measures to control the irrigation of the fertile Delta. There was always plenty of entertainment available in Cairo for the troops. The 'Music for All' building always had something going on if only a string quartet or a lone pianist, and whilst one listened to the music, one could be served with coffee or tea by white-galabieh-ed sofragi, and select from a large tray carried around on one hand by them, as many of those delectable Groppi's cakes as one could pay for or one's stomach could stand.

Back to work on the test benches, I found that I was on the 4-12 shift, but being now the senior NCO i/c, I was not actively engaged on the benches, except to keep a check on what the lads were up to. There was a constant demand for reconditioned engines; the average flying life of a Merlin in the desert was only fifty hours because of the damaging effect of the constant dust-storms either natural, or raised by aircraft on take off.

Let me give some idea of these storms. One night I was sitting at my packing case desk in the office during a fairly windy night. This office was brickbuilt as to walls but the roof was a nearly flat one of corrugated steel sheeting. Suddenly the light went out, all the papers on my desk flew off and looking up to see why the bulb had extinguished, I saw the stars where the roof had been. We found that roof about a hundred yards away, and it was very lucky that no one had intercepted its projection.

The officer in charge of the Test Section was a Flt/Lt Kelly, and a real good type he was. One day he pointed out to me a small item on casualty lists.

The Military Mission to the Royal Egyptian Air Force were asking for volunteers among sergeant fitters to act as Motor Transport Advisor. That sounded like a good idea to me, and so with Mr Kelly's blessing, I put in an application. Strange things happen in this world. I was called to Cairo for an interview, and found later, to my chagrin, that I was the only applicant.

Nevertheless, I was accepted, and told to clear myself completely from the RAF, pay, kit, the lot. What should I wear to take up my new duties? There's a house in Heliopolis, I was told, where clothing and equipment of deceased personnel, which were not wanted by their next of kin, were sold off on behalf of said next of kin. I could obtain much of what I should need from this house, which had become known as Dead Man's Gulch and the rest could be purchased at any of the shops and suchlike to be found around Cairo. To make life even easier, I was given an advance of pay to deal with these purchases.

This job carried the rank of Warrant Officer, or, as the Egyptians called it of Sôl, and the pay was commensurate, as near as I remember it was £52 per month plus a servant allowance which varied per month according to the position of the moon. Islamic countries have thirteen months of twenty-eight days I believe, which would account for this, but I never have argued about pay, just as long as I have enough to cover outgoings.

My task, if one can dignify it with that description, was to oversee a large workshop at Almaza, on the outskirts of Heliopolis, which itself is a suburb of Cairo, even if about ten miles away. In the workshop, which did the repair and maintenance for the whole of the REAF, were seven - yes, seven - foremen and their accompanying subordinates. There was also a Bash Shaweysh which rank was equivalent to our RAF Flight Sergeant who was in charge of a platoon of askaris to act as drivers etc. My desk and 'operational base' was in a small office, but within the confines of this haven there dwelt a couple of indigenous storekeeper clerks of whom more anon.

Although no indication of just what my duties were to be was ever given, either verbally or on paper, I read them as being to ensure the efficiency of the section, much as if it were a normal RAF section. In retrospect, it has dawned upon me that my brief was, probably, to keep my eyes shut to events, and go through the motions, not, as I'd imagined, the reverse!

Every morning, as I walked into my office, my two clerks would have stores indents which required my signature before the items could be drawn from the Main Stores for use in the MT repair shop. As the equipment of the REAF was in many respects identical to equipment required by the RAF, any item which the Egyptians had was so much less available for our own lads: that's how I looked at it then and nothing has changed that idea since.

After getting my sea-legs so to speak, I began to stroll around the workshops daily, and take an intelligent interest in the progress of repairs, etc. During these little wanderings, I noticed cases where items used on some jobs were being duplicated in later indent forms which I was countersigning. I began to make checks and take notes where this was occurring and to the dismay and general annoyance of both my two clerks and, eventually, the Egyptian Flt/Lt who was in overall command of the MT Section, I refused to sign requisitions for repeats of stores which had already been issued for any particular job.

Faber quisque Fortunae suae. Every man the architect of his own Fortune.

Thus was I laying the foundations of my own fortune. My unwonted - and unwanted - interferences in the process of these apparent mistakes were not well received. The handicraft skill of very many Egyptians was well adapted to motor engineering and metal-work in general; there was a thriving business locally in keeping what vehicles the civil population had in reasonably roadworthy condition. A ready supply of spare parts which could be fiddled from the only people with supply routes - us - must have been netting fair profits, before my scotch in the wheel, though it's doubtful if those profits sustained much damage overall, with the multiple possibilities there were in the Delta.

Being more or less outside Air Force jurisdiction, we members of the Military Mission had to find our own accommodation, and three of us shared a flat, for which we paid £E 20 per month, and a house servant - a young Sudanese who came every morning, brought us tea in bed, and cooked us breakfast whilst we dressed. It must have been quite distressing for him, but to us it was humorous to see this young Muslim lad frying bacon on a primus stove, with the pan held at arm's length and an expression of fear and distaste on his face as he tried to avoid being spotted by pork fat.

After we three Sybarites had departed for what, for want of a better word, we called work, in the pick-up truck which collected and returned us each day, Yussef cleaned the flat, made our beds and prepared our tiffin ready for when we finished work at midday. All the shopping except our occasional visits to the NAAFI grocery stores was done by Yussef, and all for the £E 1 per week which we paid him, plus, of course, what he fiddled out of the shopping trips, and that no doubt was much less than it would have cost us had we done our own shopping. In this, as in many other aspects of life, the labourer was worthy of his hire.

It was a good life if the health can stand the attacks on the liver: we had diplomatic privileges on the Mission, which entitled us to twelve bottles per month of either whisky or gin at eight shillings a bottle, three bottles per day of the local brew, Stella beer, any amount of Palestinian brandy, wine from a vineyard near Alexandria, Clos Matamir, at 15 piastres per bottle, and two Sabbath days a week, Friday and Sunday, when we were free to drive thirst away with all this.

When the end did come to this dissolute profligacy I was relieved more than distressed. It came about because at a party given by one of my fellow missionaries I was so annoyed by the conduct of what proved to be a fellow guest, that I hit him rather hard - and he turned out to be a friend of our Group Captain.

Not being the sort of conduct desired of a diplomat, it was thought expedient that I be replaced forthwith, and it was truly remarkable just how quickly these matters can be expedited. From my interview with Groupy, to reporting to RAF Heliopolis for kitting out RAF-wise, and being entrained at Bab-el-Hadid station bound for Benghazi, was a matter of very few days.

CHAPTER 18
Benghazi

The bare idea of lumbering myself with a complete issue kit, in addition to all the gear that I'd collected whilst with the Mission was anathema. But a solution was to be organised: reporting to the Clothing Stores at Heliopolis for kitting out, I persuaded them to issue what were known as Deficiency Chits, not just for those items which they couldn't supply, but for the whole kit including greatcoat, and all that canvas paraphernalia which was only used on rare occasions. This idea, it must be said, was practically unheard of but it had the great merit from Heliopolis's point of view of being no drain whatsoever on clothing stocks.

This left me with a kit which was, in some respects, non-standard. Obviously, the beautiful barathea tunic and slacks I'd had from Dead Man's Gulch couldn't be worn as the Sergeant to which I had so suddenly reverted, but, by stripping the barathea from the peak of my cap, to expose the patent leather beneath, and replacing the crown and laurel leaf badge for an OR cap badge, that at least could be worn. The tunic of a khaki gabardine suit which a local tailor had made, I gave to Yussef, our general factotum at the flat, but the slacks I kept; and of course, all the khaki drill stuff I'd had to buy.

I'll bet Yussef put on a good show when he wandered round the markets in that tunic, because it fitted him like a glove which is more than the issue-type battledress blouse with which I replaced it did for me.

And so I rolled up at Cairo main, Bab-el-Hadid, looking reasonably like a a normal Air Force sergeant, with the possible exception that I had no kitbag, but did have a largish camelskin suitcase with two - yes two - tennis rackets strapped on the top of it. These were to occasion a few sarcastic comments from desert-hardened squaddies during the ensuing few days' journey, but were to prove of use before being finally dumped.

The train journey along the coastal route was not exactly the height of luxury - that was not expected - but if it had not been quite so long-drawn out, to over twenty-six hours before reaching Tobruk, it would have been easier to bear for one so recently used to the luxurious flesh-pots of Heliopolis. There's a lot to be said for hard wooden slatted seats in public service vehicles and some cinemas, as they are not so likely to harbour the sort of small livestock which have no other source of food than the occupiers of such seats. The one cinema in Cairo which I visited more than once, 'The Metro', not only had full air-conditioning - so that one could stand outside on the footpath and cool down - but it had upholstered seats which were bug-free, which proved that was possible.

Arrival at Tobruk, and those of us who were destined for further afield were accommodated in a general Transit Camp at El Adem. Bell-tents! Tea that had a most peculiar taste from the brackish water it was made with, and no beer in the Sergeants' Mess. However, after a decent meal, some of us repaired to the beerless bar where the water could be disguised with orange juice and gin. With the thirst generated by a day and a night in that train, I slept rather too well on the deck in that bell-tent. When, next morning I donned my battledress blouse, which had hung on the central pole, my wallet was missing; the thief was a bit unlucky because after paying my bar bill, I'd pushed the wad of notes behind the wallet, but that important clothing chit had gone the way of all equipment which is not tied down and was to cause me a little heartburn later.

The onward journey from El Adem was to be undertaken in a 3-tonner, just half a dozen of us, four army bods and a couple of airmen, with an East African driver. Sometimes I think we should have been pushed, to say the least, to carry on any sort of war without our Empire - as it was then; wherever one went along the North African littoral, one found Empire troops. There were three hospitals in Cairo: The New Zealand General, of blessed memory, a South African Hospital for coloured SA troops, but with white nurses and doctors, and the British Army Hospital in Abbassia Barracks, where I spent a couple of weeks being cured of baccillary dysentery. There were probably other hospitals also, of which I was not - happily - aware.

This last interlude in my Egyptian Air Force time was practically self-inflicted, I came back to the flat one day and the beer had been delivered late, so I put a chunk of ice into it to make it drinkable. That ice must have been well primed with bacteria for it took two weeks' application of sulphathiazole to remove from my system. It was another sulpha drug which fixed my pneumonia, sulphanilamide.

We never hear much about those wonder drugs today, we've either developed better ones or the bugs have got used to them.

That was a long digression, similarly long ones were made on our truck run over the Jebel El Akdar to Benghazi. Three days it took us, the nights we spent lying UNDER the truck to avoid the dewfall but the worst experiences were when we had to drive down steep winding tracks and up again on the far side to cross some of the wadis where bridges had been either destroyed during the fighting, or perhaps had never existed. It's a nasty shock to the system to peer out of the back of a truck to see why you've stopped, to find that there's nothing to see except space, with the rear wheels just about to slip over the edge - the complete equanimity of our driver during those reverse turns made us wonder sometimes whether he knew the front from the back of the truck, and if he really didn't know where we were, but just followed his nose. But he did get us to Benghazi eventually, and in one piece, so we must have misjudged both his skill at the wheel and his sense of direction.

At Benghazi, there were two aerodromes in use by our forces: there was the old Italian 'drome at Berka Main and another not far out of 'town' at Benina. Lucky old me went to Berka, where on arrival I was given what seemed at first sight to be a pleasant billet, sharing a room in the old Iti barrack block with the orderly room sergeant, a Scot whom I shall refer to as Jock because I've forgotten his name and that's how I addressed him anyway.

The barracks was a two or three-storeyed building, but our room was on the ground floor, with iron bedsteads, and built-in cupboards for kit stowage. It didn't take long for me to find out that that building was practically crawling with bedbugs; no sooner were the lights out than so also were those hungry little parasites. Under canvas they can be dealt with pretty effectively, by taking all bedding out of the tent, giving the bed itself a good dosing with petrol and spraying the sand floor. To remain clear for a reasonable time, the feet of the bed are then placed in tin lids or similar, which are filled with paraffin.

This system was going to be difficult in a brick building, but Jock and I, at my instigation, tried it. We took the beds and our kit outside the block, then proceeded to paint the walls, ceiling, floor, and that damned cupboard incubator with high octane fuel: if anyone had walked into our room with a cigarette on, it's possible this would not be being written, at least by me. The whole dangerous proceeding turned out however, to be of moderate success; the building was so alive with hungry insects, that they found their way back into our pristine chamber within a very short time; and more permanent ways of avoiding being eaten alive had to found, of which more anon.

There were a couple of South African Air Force Squadrons stationed nearby, and I was attached to a small Flight in 136 MU which acted as the Headquarters Flight for their Halifaxes. This entailed engine changes and 120 hour inspections, with major repairs as necessary. Another sergeant, Taff Thomas, and myself had about eight or nine lads apiece for these tasks, and soon formed a happy group. The Merlin XX's fitted to these Halibags, were fairly easy to maintain if one followed the book, and from reading all relevant schedules when on test benches at Tura, I'd discovered that it was possible to give them a little extra punch by measuring the control linkwork lengths very accurately. A satisfying process.

I did get my self-esteem a little battered one day - a Spitfire arrived for a major inspection; it was one of the later kites and was fitted with a Merlin 72 which had an American Bendix-Stromberg carburettor. It also had a take off boost much higher than the Merlin XX's of the Halifax, which I seem to remember was 12 lbs. This Mark 72's boost was over 20lbs, and when giving the engine a ground test on the edge of the tarmac, I made the mistake of treating it like a XX and pushed the throttle to full with the result that I gave the TWO lads who were lying across the tailplane a scare almost as great as I gave myself. That Spitfire leapt over the Gerry shaped-metal chocks we had in front of the wheels and was a couple of hundred yards across the aerodrome before I could get the throttle back. It had also managed to rise above the grass for about three feet, so I must be one of very few people who have flown a Spit. without any previous instruction; it might have made me feel like Orville Wright if I'd not been so shaken.

The Sergeants' Mess at Berka was a pleasant walk from the hangars, and the route took one along the edge of a field which was lined with eucalyptus trees, a nice change from the smell of petrol, etc. The mess was situated in the buildings of an Italian farm complete with foal-yard and along one side of the yard were open-fronted implement sheds. There was plenty of timber around the camp from packing cases etc., and Jock and I set about cleaning one of the archways of this shed complex and fitting the open front with a door and a window. It took a remarkably short time, and then we only had to furnish it with beds and a table also made from packing case material: even the glazed window opened, a real home from home. It did become a little stifling at times so we tried to knock a small window into the back wall, on the outer side of which was a roughish road. We actually did succeed one afternoon, in breaking through that wall which was built like the drystone walls of Yorkshire, with a load of small stuff as filling between the outer skins. As we broke through, the draught which came in filled our nice little billet - and our eyes - with grit. It was a long time before we could bring ourselves to have another go at making a proper job of the hole which we'd stuffed rapidly with a blanket!

Much that had little to do with war happened at Benghazi. The mess cooks there had capacities outside normal requirements. One day I was wandering fairly aimlessly around the vast area where scrap Axis aircraft had been dumped when I came upon the wooden mainplane of an Italian kite, and between the upper and lower skins there was a well established hive of wild bees; at least, they seemed very wild to me when I poked my enquiring nose in. Back in the mess, I told one of our cooks of this and found that he was an apiarist. So I took him next day to show him its position whereupon he pulled the flaps of his Glengarry cap down over his ears, donned a pair of greyback socks for gloves, and proceeded to tear great lumps of comb from that mainplane until he had almost a bucketful. Meanwhile the bees were going berserk - and I was fifty feet away. The cook didn't get stung, but I did, and I didn't get any of the honey either; it's a very unfair world.

These cooks were a versatile lot; from somewhere they had scrounged a pig some time before my arrival, and it was due for the chop. Preparations were put in hand in the foal-yard just outside our little alcove home. A tea-boiler as used in field kitchens was used to boil plenty of water, an iron bathtub was gathered from some obscure source and the pig brought forth for the ritual slaughter. When the water was hot enough and transferred to the bath, our Kiwi test pilot was engaged to deliver the coup-de-grâce with his service revolver, a .45 Colt in this case. Whilst the cooks held the poor pig by the ears,

Kiwi put two of those heavyweight slugs into its brain. The result was startling: piggy shook off his/her holders and went on a mad dash around the yard, the funniest aspect of which that our Squadron Leader Padre was watching the procedure - either to bless the sacrifice, or to ensure that some pork went to the Officers' Mess. The pig took an instant dislike to being converted, and chased him round the yard until the cooks rescued him. All was not yet over with our porcine pal; the cooks decided that only the knife would effect a transformation to pork, and cut deeply with much blood after which the poor animal was thrown into the bath of hot water. They were, perhaps a little previous, because as it hit the boiling water, that pig, with two .45's in its head, and its heart lying alongside the bath, just leapt out of the bath - and collapsed on the ground. It didn't eat all THAT tough.

Some nights, Jock and I had our sleep interrupted by the noise from a pack of semi-wild dogs which roamed around the countryside, and often came quite near to the farmyard. The leader of this pack had a very individual bark, it was in waltz-time and very low pitched - 'WOUF, Wuf Wuf'.

After a few nights of this nuisance we decided to do something about it, so borrowing a .38 for Jock, and with my little .38 which I'd bought in Valletta, we went on the hunt for that scavenging pack of hounds. At least it helped us to sleep, because chasing them all over Cyrenaica made us almost too tired to curse them.

One night, when discussing these so far fruitless expeditions in the Mess, Kiwi thought he could do with a spot of practice with his .45, and decided to join us on our next hunting effort. That night was to prove somewhat hair-raising all told. On hearing the pack approaching we gathered the weapons and sallied out. That leader was a crafty old dog, and knew a thing or two about being hunted. He led us for miles, always just far enough away to encourage us to further effort, and then he stopped and the pack went quiet so that we were a bit disorientated. We spread out so that we were about fifty yards apart and crouched down in the long grass around us. This was definitely a tactical mistake; those dogs began to advance towards us with their crafty leader egging them on with that distinctive bark - from behind them too, just like the Duke of Plaza Toro in the Gondoliers. As we were lying down and thus we couldn't see each other, we couldn't fire at the dogs without risk to ourselves, but one shot in the air sent them off like the Quorn in full cry. We did have some revenge on the species as a whole. Hearing a few odd barks we traced the noise to what turned out to be a native village where the dwellings were built into a surrounding containing wall, similar to an English medieval strong-point. The barking was coming from within the village and increased as we approached, which so upset us that Kiwi climbed up onto the top of the wall and took a few pot-shots at the dogs inside, which did tend to quieten them a little.

A mention should be made of the night which, perhaps added to the above undesirable behaviour, led almost directly to the cessation of our dog-hunting peccadilloes. On one of our expeditions we were led even farther away from the usual areas and in scouting around for some indication of a homing direction, we came upon a barbed-wire fence. There seemed no way around this after a brief recce, so we crawled underneath to follow what we had decided was the general direction which we needed. Whilst we were actually trapped under this wire, we heard footsteps, and they turned out to be those of a British Army sentry, complete with one of those so-easily-fired Sten guns. We kept VERY quiet until he was well past; speaking for myself, I'd been on guard duty and could well imagine his response to sudden rustles and/or voices from the underside of a perimeter fence-wire!

Instead of retreating rapidly as wiser men would have, we continued through the wire and rose to walk calmly along the same route as the sentry. Shortly, we came to what must have been an Italian colonist's house and although by now it was about 3 a.m. there were lights showing from the windows, so we entered, and found ourselves in the ante-room or bar of some Army Mess, with several officers sitting around with drinks. It must have been nearly as great a shock to them as to us when three scruffy, muddy RAF NCO's walked into their cosy little enclave with loaded revolvers in their hands. But when we asked for directions to Benghazi they did tell us; perhaps they considered that the safest action! However, the word got round that the local administration was not well pleased at the idea of bods wandering around the countryside armed to the teeth and giving nightmares to local Arabs and others.

Within the Camp bounds were three very tall radio masts, which had survived the bombing by our Wimpies. They were square section steel towers which tapered up from concrete bases, and were perhaps two hundred feet high. An enclosed steel ladder led up to a round platform and from thereon the mast consisted of a round steel tube of about a foot in diameter with footrests welded onto it for the last thirty to forty feet.

On one never-to-be-forgotten night, after an evening in the Mess bar, I was persuaded that the view from the top of these masts was well worth the climb. It was certainly a wide-ranging view: one could see clear across the marshes to the harbour with most of the ships there being lit-up as if there were no such thing as the Luftwaffe. After the strenuous climb it was very pleasant and cool up there, and I was enjoying myself until someone below shouted up to ask how I was getting on and what could I see. Looking down to answer gave me the impression that the mast was at an angle to the vertical, and with the vibration of that slender tube from my movement, I just froze: it was a long time before I summoned enough courage to start down that mast, which was shaking almost as much as I was. Flying in an aircraft is one thing, up a pole without a parachute is quite another.

To prove that fools never learn, even from their own mistakes, I got myself into a similar situation on Pen-Yr-Olywen some years later, but that's another story.

It was about this time that I heard from my brother that he had been made up to Sergeant. He was one of those brainy elite, the Code and Cypher bods, which like war-time air-crews, were always given sergeant's tapes as their lowest rank held. He had also been posted to, of all places, Heliopolis. As I'd not seen him for nearly three years, I decided to put in for a spot of leave in the Delta. This needed some organising but there was a Wellington Squadron based at Benina who I knew sent an occasional kite to the Delta for any big repairs needed. It seemed that one was scheduled to be sent to Lydda in Palestine next day, and I was told that if I could get a pass signed, managed to get to Benina by breakfast time, and spoke nicely to the pilot he might drop me at Alexandria *en route*.

Well, I managed all that, and was away eastwards in that Wimpy, and a draughty old battlewagon it was; they might have patched up the holes in the fabric cover of the fuselage at least. Although I was grateful for the lift, that flight certainly made me very sympathetic towards those aircrew who had spent European winter nights on operations in Wimpies.

I suppose I should also express some sympathy for the obliging pilot of that particular Wellington, because in landing it at Alexandria, just for my convenience, one wheel dropped into a roughish patch, and damaged the oleo leg, so that he couldn't take off again for Lydda. I never found out whether or not he was shot for landing at that rough airfield, because, in selfish unconcern, I just dashed off and caught the train for Cairo.

After a very indulgent week with my young brother in Cairo and Heliopolis, I was supposed by all the rules to report to the RTO at Bab-el-Hadid for a place on that hard-seated train to Tobruk, and the even worse truck journey from El Adem to Benghazi. Not a very alluring prospect, so I just missed the weekly train.
"What do I do now, can I get a flip back?"
"Well, yes, but you'll have to wait for a low priority. There's an air-booking office in Cairo run jointly by the RAF Transport Command and the USAF."
There was no great hardship in having to report in Cairo at 5.30 p.m. every day, and I managed to get an extra week's leave in before a seat became available and I was told to be at the Booking office in Shari-el-Gumhuriya by that midnight.
There was still quite a wait before take off, but the Dakota I'd been allotted a seat in did take off in darkness; it was only as we climbed to operating height through the dawn cloud cover that the real beauty of flying at that time of day hit me. The sky above the clouds was all colours from deep orange and crimson through green to a dark blue and still blackish to the west, with the whole of the colours being transferred to the cloud layer below us.
Apart from the wonder of that first half hour, the flight was uneventful if one forgets the effect on my nerves as I watched the tips of the mainplane flapping up and down about three feet as we flew in the turbulent air over the Jebel-el-Akdar mountains.

There was some disapproving reaction from our disciplinary Flight Sergeant over my managing to fiddle an extra week's leave, but nothing permanently damaging occurred although he did express some desire that I should wear a standard glengarry instead of my secondhand WO's cap. When he insisted, it was as well that whilst I'd been in Heliopolis, I had managed to replace the chit which had been stolen at El Adem. To obtain a deficiency chit for a complete kit was fairly rare, to obtain TWO in fairly quick succession was not far short of miraculous.

Very soon after that extended leave, the two SAAF Halifax Squadrons were moved to Algeria, leaving Taff Thomas and I very little work to keep us occupied. But those South Africans knew when they'd had good service and it was not long before they actually sent a Liberator to collect Taff and me and our little gang of lads.

CHAPTER 19
Algeria

It was all very much a stimulus to our egos for the SAAF to send the Liberator for us, but the trip itself was not exactly luxurious even though the Liberator was one of those the RAF had adapted as transport aircraft. To add to the lack of enjoyment, we took off fairly late at night and were flying over the Mediterranean until we landed just before dawn at an airfield near Tunis. This airfield was furnished with a temporary runway constructed with those interlocking steel sheets known as Summerfield Tracking: the noise which emanated from the contact of our undercart with that runway made me, at least, think that we had forgotten to put the wheels down.

By chance, a Dakota landed there just after we did, and who should stagger out of it and be sick on the grass but the Sweetheart of the Forces; poor lass must have had a rough flight over France from Blighty.

On our arrival at Maison Blanche, which was about ten miles from the city of Algiers, Taff and I found ourselves billeted in a corrugated steel hut, very similar to a Nissen hut but several times larger; and we were to find that in summer heat it would be several times hotter too.

True to the generally practised form of the RAF of posting personnel where they least wanted to go, and employing them in jobs they were least qualified to do, we found at that 144 MU, that despite the requests - or because of them - of the SAAF, our close-knit little party were split up. To cap that, I personally was allotted the job of i/c dismantling bay at the reception end of an engine repair 'factory'. The engines on which this ERS operated were Pratt & Whitney double-row radials, 1800 and 2800 cu in. used in Daks, etc. Well, it's all experience I thought, and got on with it. All the parts had to be cleaned of course, before passing to the various inspection bays for checking prior to re-assembly, and for this sand-blasting and generally dirty task, I had, in addition to RAF bods, a number of local Algerian labourers whose foreman was an ex-sergeant of the French colonial forces, and a fierce-looking gentleman he was with his great bushy moustache. This ex-Goum type rode to work each day in style on a stallion, which he tethered on a patch of wasteland nearby. It was a daily amusement to watch this unfortunate animal with the sun on his back and the long grass tickling his stomach as he moved about to graze; the combination causing him to be sexually aroused intermittently.

Algiers, in contrast to Benghazi and most points East (with the exception of Cairo of course), was a city of some culture as regards entertainments for the troops. Entertainments, which were in most cases laid on for the civilian population, but which were to some extent available to troops. For instance, there was a resident operatic repertory company 'operating' in the theatre and when I discovered this, I usually managed at least one visit per week, and occasionally two.

I don't fully recall when, but in wandering around during free time, Taff and myself discovered the remains of a country club, complete with swimming pool and tennis courts. The buildings were wrecks, the pool was empty of water, and full of rubbish but one court was usable - and still had a semblance of a net extant. The two rackets which had given some army types such amusement now came into their own. Whenever duty allowed, Taff and I had a good bash there, but we had to return to camp to shower.

It was during one of these off duty 'get fit' episodes that we experienced a locust swarm. There were just a few advance party insects to begin with, which we more or less ignored, then gradually, the air became absolutely full of these four-inch jobs, with their rustling wings. Looking upwards, was just like looking up during a snowstorm, when the flakes look black against the sky. Taff and I packed up playing tennis and just batted at these hordes until we were surrounded by corpses, and the rackets as well as ourselves were liberally bespattered with their yellow fluids. After about half an hour of passage, the last of them disappeared northward and probably perished somewhere in the Mediterranean and we pair of idiots certainly were in need a shower that day.

An interesting thing about that deserted club was the large number of swallows' nests there were all around the eaves: I was aware that they flew south at the end of our summer, but it had not occurred to me that they travelled that far, and that they had nests there which meant that they had two clutches per year.

Another form of sport which was available in Algeria was horse-racing; it was here that I first met with that dangerous looking racing where high-stepping trotters pulled lightweight curricles at speeds which defied belief.

Then there was the system in use, whereby a 'responsible' senior NCO could hire an Air Force vehicle on what was known as a repayment basis, and take his section - or perhaps just a group - out for the day to places like the village of Forte de l'Eau which had a splendid beach for swimming and loafing, even if it was littered with abandoned Landing Craft Tank etc., left behind after the 'Torch' landings.

There was also the possibility of ski-ing and/or tobogganing in the Atlas Mountains, which were only forty-odd miles away across the fertile coastal plain. I took my lads from the test benches for a weekend trip to this venue, in a pick-up truck with canvas cover and remember their cries of woe as we wound our way up a winding road between high snow walls. As we swung round each bend of the hairpin road, the effect was, apparently, to make them seasick. Yours truly, of course, was comfortably ensconced in the cab and felt none of these unsettling sensations. It was, nonetheless, a very pleasant weekend away from the roar of aero-engines. A reminder of that trip is the propeller boss which I collected from the airscrew repair unit at Blida on the route back to Maison Blanche; an item of aviation interest which I had always coveted.

Eventually, the RAF took pity on us being cooked in that large tin shack, and we were moved to what had in some time past, been the married quarters of a French Armée, or Armée d'Air unit, at Maison Carré, which was about half-way between the 'drome and Algiers. The eponymous Maison Carré was a prison which was surrounded - as the name might indicate - by a high wall covering some four acres. Between the prison and our camp was a region of bare ground about one hundred yards wide, which we had to cross to reach the main road from the aerodrome to Algiers.

The actual permanent married quarters which some NCO's occupied were fairly good wooden hut-type buildings, but the 'overflow' - of which I was one - made do by sharing fourteen foot E.P.I.P. tents, in the spaces between. The whole camp was surrounded by a high wire fence, re-enforced by the usual barbed wire coils and in addition the camp was patrolled by sentries armed with that frightening weapon, the Sten gun.

One night, a very enterprising local raider cut his way through that formidable wire, and also through the wall of my tent; he took most of my kit, which included my camera, all the photographs of three years past - plus negatives - my .38 revolver, much kit, even including the clothes I had been wearing the day before but - bearing in mind the sharpness of the knife which cut into the tent - he left me my life. Not that I was very grateful at the time: for some weeks afterwards, I scoured the Arab markets in the Muskis of the casbah looking for traces of my possessions such as the leather suitcase and a buffalo-horn handled knife which one of my askaris had presented me with when I left the Egyptian A.F. This casbah was out of bounds to British troops for obvious reasons, so it was probably just as well that I found no recognisable trace of the booty.

There had been what was known as an English Hospital in Algiers in pre-war days; just another of those outposts of Empire which post-war politicians have rendered impossible to maintain. The staff of this establishment, an English girl, and her colleague, a Spaniard, had remained there during the German occupation, and while I was in Algeria, stayed on as hostesses when the RAF took over the building as a rest-camp for senior NCO'S. It became a regular port of call for me, when in Algiers. It turned out in conversation, that the Spanish lady, Maria Veliesid, shared a birthday with me - in addition to a marked appreciation of South African brandy! - even though she was, indeed, just twice my age at that time.

Despite all these manifest attractions, it seemed to me that it was time that I moved on and took a more exciting part in this argument with Gerry. What really prompted these feelings was probably a letter I received from my brother, who by this time was in Italy. His job there was to liaise with the forward units of the Desert Air Force and the Eighth Army. To this effect he had a radio truck, a driver, and a pair of binoculars. When our lads found an objective which was being a bit insuperable, they contacted him, and it was then his job to bring up the Kittihawk Fighter/Bombers and direct them onto the offending objective. With a task like that one could actually see the effects of one's war effort.

I applied forthwith for a posting to Italy, in order to be with my brother, but found that there was no chance of this. I could however, if we wanted to be together, 'claim' him to be with me in Algiers.

After a bit of heart-searching and form-filling we decided that might not be a bad idea: how wrong can one be?

A story which Frank told me during one of the long sessions we had together is illustrative of the interesting life which we had curtailed by our 'claiming'. He and his driver came to a village which had seen quite a bit of action, and was so damaged as to be completely deserted by its Italian population. They found a dilapidated house which had a semblance of a roof and decided to leaguer there for the night. There were no wooden parts left in the house which could be used to make a fire to keep out the winter, and they had just made up their minds to grin and bear it when they heard that clanking that tanks make when on the move. The radio truck was in the yard of the house and fairly obscure from the road, so they kept their heads down and hoped for the best. When the 'tank' appeared it turned out to be no less than a British sapper with a bulldozer! This solitary hero was welcomed with open arms, for in the immediate vicinity of the house stood a solitary olive tree. The sapper was prevailed upon to bulldoze this tree out of the ground as a price of sharing the accommodation, which proved almost too easy; but when it came to chopping it up to fit into the fireplace, the 'dozer was used to push it through a wall of the house so that the branches broke off during the process. Unfortunately, that building had already had a rather rough time and was not up to further assailments; there was a devastating rumble and the whole place collapsed on top of the bulldozer so that the three of them then had neither fireplace nor roof for the night.

Not long after Frank came to North Africa, the Gerries finally saw sense and left the further attempts to beat the combined forces of the Allies to their friends the Japs.

We had a couple of ex-Africa Corps POW's working in the Sergeants' Mess at Maison Carré, and they didn't take kindly to the idea of VE Day. To them the whole story was just propaganda: no-one could possibly beat the Wehrmacht. Well, they eventually found out differently!

A more serious result of the glad news was that the indigenous Algerians decided that if they were going to get rid of the French, now would be a good time and there was an uprising inland, with much murder and mayhem occurring. It didn't take the French long to put down the insurrection, with the aid, first of Lockheed Lightning Fighters borrowed from the US and a few Dakota-loads of the Foreign Legion. It would be some years before the Algerians would try such freedom efforts again, but the next time proved more permanently successful.

There seemed to be a general air of unrest in the country as a whole, which had been exacerbated by the recent rising and the remorseless manner of its apparent termination. Naturally, this atmosphere in the area of our own operations was not considered conducive to long life, if one should stray beyond the limits of one's unit after dark: there were, indeed several cases of soldiers being attacked, and left, not only stripped of their clothing, but dead, too.

During the actual uprising, and its bloody sequel, we at 144 MU were confined to camp for two or three days as a precaution, but this could not be continued indefinitely. In that summer of '44, there was also an outbreak of bubonic plague in Algiers which caused a widespread confinement to barracks; but that strangely enough, was much more cheerfully put up with.

The French colonists had had a system of rationing of clothing and foods similar, one supposes, to the system operated in Blighty; but their system was not extended to the indigenes, which left the local Arabs and Berbers with few, if any, options in clothing themselves, and no doubt also curtailed their food intake somewhat. It was no wonder then that they took chances when presented with a soft touch - or even a not so soft one - to obtain a decent set of khaki serge.

Chances must have been taken once too often for some unlucky types: it was a commonplace sound, in early mornings, to hear a firing squad ending the careers of transgressors in that high-wall enclosed Maison Carré Prison.

My task in the factory soon became so boring that when the sergeant i/c test-benches was posted away, I immediately volunteered myself for the job and with that previous experience at Tura-el-Asmant with 111 MU, there was no opposition. It was during the Bubonic Scare that we found a nest of rats were living comfortably beneath our T/B office - which was in fact the discarded packing case in which a P 47 Thunderbolt had arrived. To rid ourselves of these possible carriers of the disease, we sealed up the area beneath the office with sand-bags and by using a length of rubber tubing, directed the exhaust gases from our three-tonner into the space. The operation was quite successful with regard to the demise of the rat colony but it occurred to us later that the fleas which are the actual carriers to man might perhaps be immune to carbon monoxide etc. For a week or so we kept a lively check for any swellings in the armpit!

One fault, and that the most often occurring fault with the P & W engines which the workshops turned out and sent to me for test-running was a natural propensity to use more oil than they were supposed to. Natural because, even after an overhaul, they were suffering the effects of flying from airfields which were either muddy in wet weather, or threw up clouds of abrasive dust in dry weather. The oil consumption could have been rectified by fitting new rings to the pistons in many cases, but the supply of spares was not able to keep up with the demand.

There were frequent altercations between myself and the Flt. Lt i/c the whole workshop about what he described as my unwillingness to co-operate in passing off more engines. I was, it later proved, labouring under the mistaken idea that lads were going to have to fly behind these engines and it was my job to see that they didn't fall to pieces in the air.

I found out later that the engines which DID pass were being delivered to another MU in the Algiers area whence most of them were being taken out into Algiers Bay in a specially adapted barge - and just jettisoned, case and all! There's always the possibility that this was dud gen, but it has the ring of truth to me when one considers that we are still paying for the Lease/Lend scheme of those war-time years, and add that the Dakota-equipped Transport Unit based at Maison Blanche absolutely refused to accept any of our engines when replacements were needed.

Wandering into the CO's office one day in his absence, I noted a letter from Group informing him that one of our pairs of test benches should be dismantled, and packed into cases for onward transmission to the Far East theatre of war but although the letter was about a week old, he had not said anything about this job to date.

The benches we were using at Maison Blanche were much more 'refined' than those at Cairo, which were an old Heenan type, where the tester stood behind a wooden shield which carried the instrumentation, with the draught from the fan blowing around his ears. At MB the operator was ensconced in a strong cabin with side windows through which he could see the engines on test on either side. Usually, we were testing one whilst fitters were installing another on the other side. Instead of measuring the oil used by volume as in Egypt, the oil tank was permanently fitted to a weighing gadget so that there was a constant check. Also, and this sometimes worked to our disadvantage, the boost pressure was taken direct from a mercury-filled 'U' tube instead of a bourdon tube gauge. Much more accurate of course, but the tester had to remember to isolate the manometer tube before acceleration tests, otherwise the surging of the mercury caused it to shoot out, hit the roof of the cabin, and descend in a heavyweight shower on the tester and disappear into a myriad of small silver globules all over the deck!

After reading that letter in the office, I expected any moment to be given the instructions it contained, but all we had on the benches were the usual complaints when engines were rejected for high oil consumption and sent back to the workshop. So I decided to get on with the task. There was a large dump of timber available on the 'drome left from when so many aircraft had been brought there direct from the U.S. of A. and it was not a greatly difficult task to dismantle one pair of benches, to pack the parts into packing cases with detailed lists of the contents of each. A fairly large snag was that the fuel tank for the pair had been buried - and encased - in solid concrete. Then I remembered that I'd seen a pneumatic rock-drilling unit up on the 'drome when I'd been exchanging a few bottles of Scotch for a case or so of hickory smoked bacon (exchanges of rations between Allies and sometimes enemies, was not an unusual means of varying the diet).

When I bowled up to the hangar and asked if I might borrow this gadget, there was no hesitation and within half an hour of my asking, there appeared at the benches this vehicle driven by an Italian P.O.W. Behind the cab was a large air compressor and a reservoir; along the sides were lockers containing every possible tool which could be operated by compressed air including the road-drill which I needed. Mind you, that concrete had been well made: it took longer to dig out that fuel tank and pack it into a case than it took to dismantle and pack the whole of the rest of the bench.

The whole job was finished and ready for onward transport before there was a phone call from the Flt. Lt. telling me of the order I'd seen, and giving me just two days to do the job! A job which it had taken over a week to complete! I've often wondered whether he'd just forgotten the letter, or whether the whole exercise was a deliberate attempt to drop me in it; I'll never know.

One thing I know, my brother Frank was posted to INDIA soon afterwards, with leave in Blighty en route, and I was posted to ITALY, where I'd been trying to get for nearly a year until Frank joined me in Algeria. But, as I think I've said before, that's the way the RAF operates, and if you can't take a joke, you shouldn't have joined!

CHAPTER 20
Goodbye Algeria

Having seen Frank off to India, via his Blighty leave, the first thing I did was to apply for a posting to the Far East. Of course I should have known better, but it was always worth a try. By this time there had evolved a system of release numbers, based on age and length of service, which constituted a priority list for demobilisation, or release to the Reserve. When volunteering for the Far East, I was told that I would not have enough time to serve before release unless I signed on for an extra eighteen months at least, over and above my possible date of release.

Very shortly after signing up for this extra service the posting for Italy came through, and I found myself embarked in an Italian cruise ship, sailing eastward, but only as far as Taranto in 'sunny' Italy. This was a bit of a blow because I had been planning a birthday party with Maria, my Spanish fellow Cancerian, for the middle of July and this was now well clobbered.

In Taranto, a group of us were billeted in an hotel, which, in addition to a well-stocked bar, had a large balcony leading off from it which was on the shore of, and facing, that harbour which the Swordfish had raided so very effectively in '41.

Here we were to wait until transport could be arranged to wherever we might be destined. We, certainly myself, didn't have a clue where that would be, and it didn't seem to matter much. After a year or so of being constantly on the move, one grows a protective skin over one's consciousness but the skin was to wear a little thin at one point in THIS trip.

I forget just how long we were to stay in this holiday inn, but I recall one day we were given a ride to a glorious beach in the instep of Italy, where the water was about 60° F and as clear as crystal. That swim was fine, but the swim that several of us took on our first night in Taranto almost put us off swimming permanently. After dinner we retired to the bar and there met a wine which was new to us after the Alicante stuff we'd been used to in Algiers. A lovely brown liquid that slid down very easily, that Marsala must have had an alcohol content around 15% from its effect both then and the following morning.

It was the evening effect, with an air temperature in the seventies and our stomachs and heads full of this heavy wine, that made us wander out to the balcony. There we saw a group of happy Italian kids disporting themselves in the water of the harbour. They had a forty gallon drum there which was just awash and were using this as a diving platform. Just below our balcony there was a narrow beach of about six feet width, and it didn't take much effort for us to drop down the ten feet or so to this, strip off, and join the kids in the cooling water. Somewhere along the harbour side we could hear the strains of an orchestra at some restaurant, playing, of all tunes, 'Back to Sorrento'.

However, when the cooling was complete and the thirst returned, we found that the only way back to our bar was to walk along the beach until we could make our way to the road, and back through the front of the hotel. It was as well that it was late at night and dark, because, having no towels, we just carried our kit. The devastating sequel to this small adventure occurred after breakfast next morning. Repairing to that balcony for a cigarette and coffee, we were aghast to notice that an open sewer was disgorging its contents by the side of the hotel, and various examples of Admiral Brown's Navy were sailing past the place where we had been swimming only a few hours before.

All too soon, we had to leave this life of leisure, and were trucked over to Bari on the Adriatic Coast. Here, we were introduced to three aeroplanes which were to take us up the coast to Udine in the north. The snag as far as I was concerned was the aircraft; they were those Marauders, a large fuselage with two massive P & W Double Wasps attached, but very little wing to carry all this. That may be slightly unfair, because they were a useful kite even if they did need about two miles in which to take off.

Balancing our group and their kits, which included full toolboxes, took some ingenuity, and I managed to place my extra heavy toolbox in one aircraft and myself in another but all were about even and off we went. Well, two of the kites made it into the air eventually, the third, which contained neither me nor my kit, ran out of runway before becoming airborne, although it didn't look too serious as we looked down. I saw very little more of Italy until we landed on the field at Udine because we flew well off the coast up the Adriatic.

At Udine I found myself on yet another MU, No. 380, and one with the far from usual task of collecting surplus aircraft and vehicles from squadrons and other units which it seemed were being disbanded as 'no longer required for the propagation of the war effort'.

The personnel of these units, I suppose, were either being posted to points east, where we still had those Japs to deal with, or were on their way home. The same applied to the aircraft which covered a large area of the 'drome and surrounding agricultural land: the perimeter track looked like the carpark for an important race-meeting, with trucks and other MT of all types and condition, double-parked along it so that there was only single line traffic possible for the most part.

The personnel of 380 MU were billeted in an Italian barracks on the edge of the town, and I soon found a nice little room which I shared with a sergeant of the MT section. We became good friends and spent many evenings either in the Mess or around Udine. I was a bit devastated some years after the war to read in a newspaper that Sergeant Bill Prytherch had been electrocuted whilst he was operating a Coles crane! Apparently, the jib came into contact with overhead HT cables.

On one occasion I did get into his bad books: I'd heard that my old mob, 18 Squadron, were operating somewhere about ten miles away and borrowed one of his Jeeps for a run over to them. Unfortunately I took the wrong Jeep, one which was in for overhaul. It certainly needed overhauling after my return, for the main and big-end bearings were kaput from lack of oil, as it had been drained ready for refilling.

Because many men then serving in the RAF had joined at eighteen or thereabouts, the Air Ministry decided to try to make them useful peace-time citizens. To this end they instituted what was known as EVT (educational and vocational training). The RAF itself was my chosen future career, but I couldn't miss the chance of a good skive, so put in for driving lessons.

The MT Sergeant who took me for my first lesson did it with one of those American bomb-loading vehicles which had an extending gantry affair on the back which was used to lift the bomb, traverse it forward and lower it onto the truck. The truck also had a gearbox with six forward and two reverse gears, all of them non-synchromesh and needing double declutch changes.

My short time with the Egyptian Motor Transport section now came in very useful for most of the vehicles they had in service were 'gate crash' type gear boxes. After just a few miles with that bomb-loader, I was ringing the changes through that box as if it were fully synchromesh. This turned out to be my undoing. What I had planned was a few trips out into the local countryside, calling at various trattoria etc., as a relief from servicing aircraft in which I had no proprietorial interest: what I got was a commendation on my driving - and a request to join the team of instructors. It didn't occur to me at the time to refuse the offer and in short time I was lumbered with a pupil and a Ford three-tonner as teaching weapon. Weapon it nearly proved to be; after a gentle drive around the peri-track to give my pupil the basics, in my ignorance of the best methods of instruction, I let him take my place at the wheel with instructions to stay at low speed because of the hundreds of parked vehicles on either side of the peri-track, and to practise changing from first to second gear, up and down until it became second nature. Had he done that we should both have become rather bored no doubt, but he didn't - with a very few circuits of the 'drome, the speed rose appreciably to the point when the engine complained, which prompted my maniacal pupil to change up to third and really give it the gun. My authority as instructor counted for nothing thereafter - he could drive he thought, this is a piece of cake. The space left between serried ranks of trucks was really not sufficient for such antics but when we approached a really constricted area, and I told him to stop, it failed to register, and I was left with the only remedy, switch off and pull hard on the hand-brake. Such an experience told me that there was going to be little future for me as a driving instructor, and I took Ford and pupil straight back to the MT office and told them that I resigned forthwith from my new job. Flying was one thing, but tearing around in trucks with stupid pupils was quite another.

Actually, I was to get quite enough driving because the aircraft were so spread out on the 'drome, and I had one of those ubiquitous Morris six-wheelers as a mobile office to keep the Form 700's of the kites and ferry the lads about with.

As Gerry had retreated from our advances through Italy and southern Austria, so also had he retreated from the Russian forces advancing westward. Much of Italy was denuded of easily transportable goods by retreating Gerries and probably also by opportunist Italians, but the main sufferer of this looting was Austria, and this by the advancing Russians. It became a major part of the work of the occupying forces to ensure that the populations of Italy and that southern portion of Austria up to Vienna didn't starve.

To this end the roads from the south of Italy became filled with Allied trucks carrying consumer goods and food from the south right through to Vienna.

One of the drivers on this task came through Udine regularly with all sorts of loads for Austria; I remember one load of blankets, and another which rather amazed me of caustic soda crystals in five gallon drums. I still can't think what they needed that for when they were short of so much else.

When this driver, Jack Braithwaite, passed through northwards, I often hitched a lift with him as far as Klagenfurt in Karinthia, where there was a hotel on the Wörthersee at Krumpendorf which had been taken over as a rest camp for RAF senior NCO's. On his route back to Italy, he'd stop and collect me from this very cosy billet.

One weekend we went to Venice in that great ten-ton Mack of his, and parked it in the front garden of a villa in Mestre, whilst we stayed in some luxury at a hotel in Lido which the NAAFI had commandeered and re-named the Churchill Club.

That seemed to be the pattern of occupying forces; on another occasion we went in the Mack to Trieste, and there the local Fascist headquarters had been turned into a NAAFI hostel, and very nice too.

Not much here about work and the war effort; since VE day, the spark seemed to have gone out of most troops and they either wanted to go home to the wife and kids - or to Mum - or they wanted to get eastwards and finish the whole thing off. Little thought seemed to have been taken regarding post-war times, or mayhap I missed the point sometimes. For instance, we had a fine collection of those lightweight spotter aircraft, the Auster, which were parked in a long row along the edge of a field of marrows. One day we had one of those terrific thunderstorms which occur in northern Italy when the hailstones were literally as large as golf balls, and the fabric skins of those serviceable aircraft were reduced to shreds. Nearly fifty otherwise serviceable aircraft were scrapped because it was not considered worthwhile recovering the mainplanes. A lot of the marrows were also pulped, but the Ities salvaged most of those.

I particularly remember that storm, because I was in the Mess during it and the building was struck by lightning. There was a water pipe running along one long wall from the bar to the toilets at the other end and that pipe grew a shimmering blue haze around it which seemed to last for at least half a minute, and when it faded there was left a peculiar chemical kind of smell.

Those trips over the Julischen Alpen into Karinthia were looked forward to with pleasure. I recall one episode which occurred whilst I was there, in which a group of us RAF bods were sunning ourselves on the shore of the Wörthersee. There was also a party of Austrians near to us on this grassy area which belonged to the Krumpendorferhof where we were staying.

Floating down the lake about a mile out from our shore there appeared what looked Ike a small island, which prompted a general discussion about its nature among both groups. One of the Austrians, a typical Aryan, with golden skin and blonde-plaited pigtails, took off like a torpedo from a Swordfish and started swimming out to investigate the 'island'.

When it seemed to us that she was going a bit far out for safety, I dived into the adjacent boathouse belonging to the Gasthof and rowed madly out into the lake to effect the rescue which I thought (and perhaps hoped) might be needed. The girl, and me in the boat, arrived at the floating object more or less together, to discover that it was but a tangled mass of vegetation, myself in a hot and sweaty condition, to be greeted by that cool blonde bombshell with, "You need not have bothered, I swim quite well, thank you," in English.

Subsequent exchanges elicited that she was a ballet dancer from Graz, then employed by ENSA, a N.A.A.F.I. organisation for entertaining British troops. A lass this, who refused to be seen even talking to one of those 'Engländer' invaders, but didn't, in the event, object to walking around with one on dark evenings and telling me how marvellous the Nazis were. During war-time, as ever, one learns to accept small mercies gratefully.

As is usual in the well-wooded regions of Austria, it was the practice of this Gasthof to cut logs during the late summer months and stack them around the outer walls under wide eaves, so that they would be on hand when winter set in as it does there. In winter the

Wörthersee is so deeply frozen that the ferry boats which ply along it are replaced by motor buses.

One weekend a group of us went out with the Austrian proprietor to fell trees and bring in a load of logs. I fear that this expedition was doomed to be of little avail in heating him and his guests that winter, for the first fir tree we dropped fell right against a British Army telephone pole and brought down all the lines among its branches. Needless to say, we stayed not to assure our compatriots that it was an accident.

It was difficult not to be sympathetic towards the defeated natives; they must have had a very rough time when the Russkis moved in before we took over. I saw some very nice shoes in the window of a shop in Klagenfurt, and went inside with the object of buying a pair, to be told that what was in the window was their whole stock, they had been stripped out by the Red Army; while I took this with a pinch of salt considering that the shop was open for some sort of business, I saw their point and didn't pursue the matter.

It soon came to my turn for repatriation and true to form, I nearly missed it because I was in Klagenfurt on a week's leave (official) when the boat came in. It was only the kind offices of one of those aid drivers who called in at Krumpendorf to tell me the glad news that saved the day. The next hour or so was spent sitting on a bench outside the Gasthof, keeping a lookout for a lift back to Udine. Had I missed the boat, I might have joined the local ballet troop.

CHAPTER 21
Homeward Bound

Since the cessation of hostilities in Europe (VE Day), the Forces Mail Services had been carrying an extra burden by reason of my unloading of a lot of surplus gear which I seemed to have accrued. Most of this was books, but included a few items of touristy goods such as a silver embossed copper bowl which I'd picked up in the muski at Algier when seeking my own stolen kit.

A typewriter which I'd bought in Cairo so that the airgraphs I sent home would be readable when photographically condensed, I had sold in Italy for 40,000 lira, which was almost exactly the equivalent of the £E 20 I'd paid for it. Culture and the arts were obviously at a discount in immediately post-war Italy; I could have been paid more for a few cans of bully beef or a Jeep tyre.

Throughout most of this four year sojourn ex-Blighty I had been writing regularly to my mother more or less in diary form with, of course, due regard to the possibility of any mail getting into the hands of the enemy. I had asked her to keep all my letters until I returned home - a magnificent confidence here in my immortality - when I planned to use them as a basis for just such an account as this present work is. That the task is only now, after over fifty years have passed, being attempted, and purely from memory, due to the fact that my mother burnt those hundred or so letters just after I returned to camp after my first home leave, on the grounds that now she had me back she didn't need my letters. I was both flattered and shattered by this, but it put paid to any literary ambitions that I had then.

That diversion past; after the usual clearance chits etc., from Udine, the route home began by the ubiquitous three-tonner, via Treviso and Verona. This last town was then an almost completely walled city which must have been not greatly different from when Shakespeare's Two Gentlemen lived there; I don't doubt that by now it will be surrounded by holiday villas and/or tower blocks as so many places are.

From Brescia we travelled along one of Mussolini's autostrada to Milano, and a roughish ride that was with the two-lane concrete surface really broken up by the last couple of years' war traffic.

We spent one night en route in some Italian villa which I recall had a marble pillared colonnade along its frontal aspect, but I forget exactly where it was.

Milano was a surprise; the main railway station where we were actually expected to spend the night in the train which was to take us on the next leg of our journey was a magnificent building which could have served well as a cathedral, had they not built an even more imposing one near enough for us to visit during a quick tour of the city that first evening.

The train eventually steamed out of Milano and rolled up the miles through northern Italy to the little station of Domodossola, where we waited some time before passing through the Simplon Tunnel. When we emerged we were in Switzerland, another country in the odyssey, where we skirted Geneva and Lake Léman before entering France, but never set foot on land. That next night we spent still in the train, lying in a siding just outside Paris, before pushing on to Calais.

Here we did detrain and spent some time at a transit camp waiting for a boat. When we finally moved it was on our own two feet at last; we marched to the dock where our sea transport was lying against the wall, and had to carry our kit with us. Why not you may think, but I had gathered quite a collection over the years, despite the thieves of Algiers and the amount sent on via the mails: more than I could actually carry at one time, so I split it into two and worked a relay alongside the marching party running back to fetch the kit left behind, and thus I arrived at the quay with all kit at the same time as the rest; but not half so fresh as them.

Time must have been short, for we were taken aboard immediately, up a narrow gangway which sloped quite steeply to the quay. Once on deck I tried to get down again to fetch my second pile, but the gangplank was too narrow for travel both ways, and when the last man made the way clear - the crew pulled up the plank and I had the mortification of seeing half my kit standing on the dock. This was the second time I had left France during that war and left most of my kit behind.

That first departure from France had ended at Falmouth, where the Customs bods didn't even show an interest in the Lee Enfield I carried, never mind the kitbag full of tobacco products. At Dover, it was somewhat different. There was an Army Lieutenant just in front me as we passed through the shed, and he had one of those 120 bass accordions in addition to his personal kit. The customs officer said, "Where did you get this?" to receive the pat reply, "Oh, I took that out with me." A quick glance over the instrument, and then came, "I don't think so, that'll be £27 to pay."

It must have been even more of a blow to the Army type, than that I'd had leaving kit on the quay, because, when no money was forthcoming, that instrument was slid under the counter smartly - and I was next in line.

"What've you got in that kit bag then?"

"Just a few fags and a couple of bottles," I replied.

"Let's see them, then."

"There's a small suitcase inside the bag with my kit packed round it, it would take all day to repack that lot," I pleaded.

With my obviously innocent look, he actually let me get away with it, and to think what I MAY have been carrying.

There was little delay or fuss about an almost immediately granted leave pass, and for a whole month at that. The first thing (almost) that I did was to buy myself a motorcycle, and that was one of the new Teledraulic-forked Matchlesses, just on the market. Perhaps it would have been better for my future career in the RAF if I'd not bought it, as will transpire.

At the end of my leave I was posted to-yet another MU, this time No. 58, at Newark. There was no aerodrome at Newark that I ever saw, but the unit was also based at a hamlet just outside Lincoln at Skellingthorpe. I don't recall how long I was actually at Newark, but it was very short; perhaps because my first experience was not very good. Arriving on my bike, I found the Sergeants' Mess deserted, and after a quick meal, felt like a beer, but no mess caterer Sgt to serve it. The only senior NCO in camp was the orderly sergeant, all the rest were living out with their wives or whatever, and I was to discover very soon, that that was how it had been for a long time. One day someone was telling me of the terrible hardships they had endured when out on crash parties - which was what this Unit had been engaged in for most of the war.

To cap my unpopularity, the CO of the Unit was also the proud owner of a motorcycle, and to my astonishment - which remains to this day - he took some exception to my bike, possibly because his

ES2 Norton was fitted with girder type front forks and told me to get THAT machine off the Station.

Shortly after this altercation, the Japs decided to pack it in, and the RAF decided that it was overstaffed: anyone who had signed for extra service over and above their release number date could rescind such offers to serve His Majesty.

To my relief at the time, but to an oft recurring regret since, I took up the offer, and in a remarkably short space of time I was a semi-civilian, with never an aircraft in sight.

I say semi-civilian because once one has spent a few years in one of the Services there is something engendered in one which colours almost every subsequent action. It may be that the reconstructed Latin title of this work might almost have been 'Semper in Excreta' with some justification, yet it could also be entitled 'A Dozen of the Best', for they were indeed twelve very good years.